LEONARDO DA VINCI *A life in drawing*

200 *works from the Royal Collection*

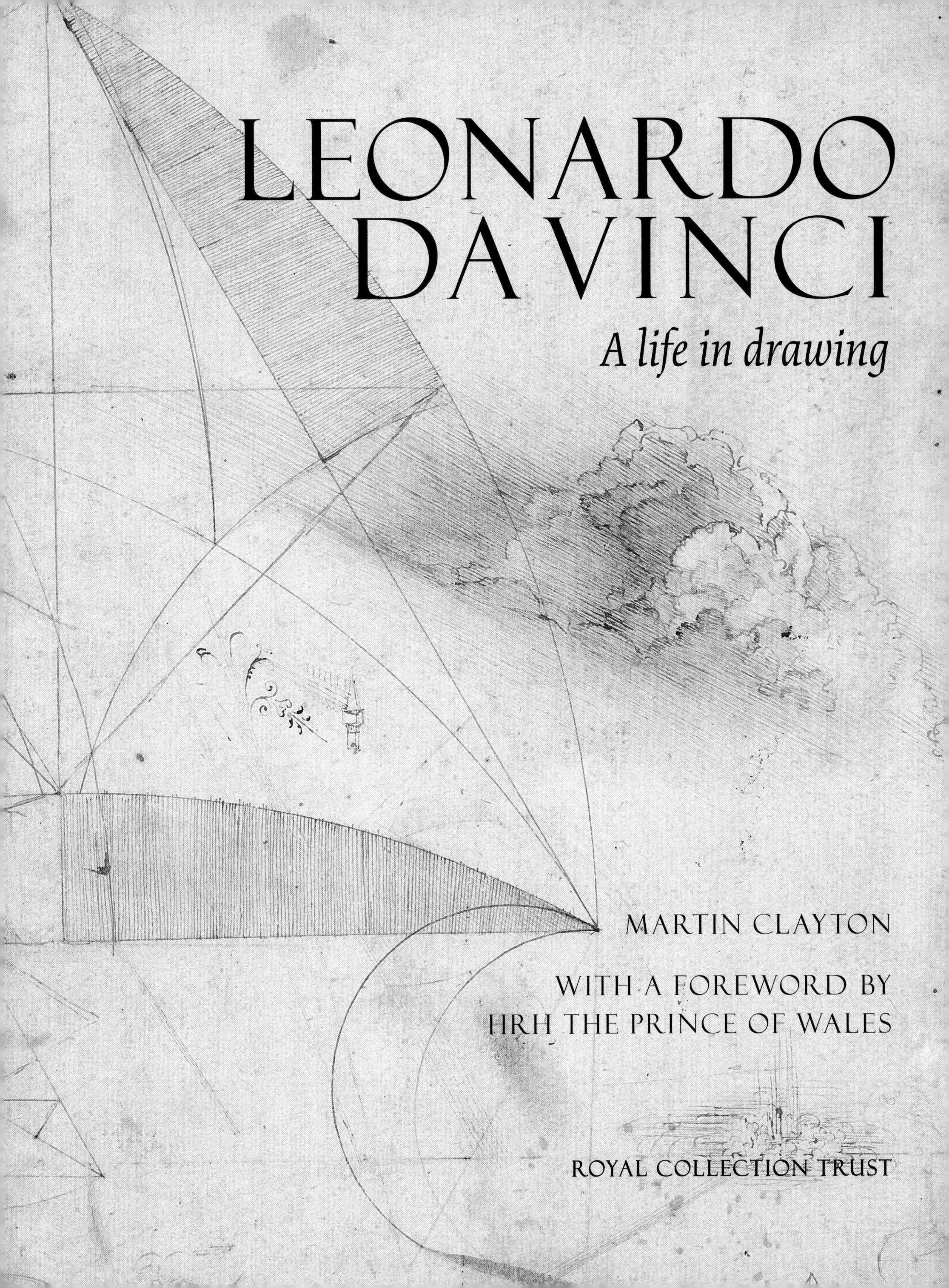

LEONARDO DA VINCI

A life in drawing

MARTIN CLAYTON

WITH A FOREWORD BY
HRH THE PRINCE OF WALES

ROYAL COLLECTION TRUST

Contents

CLARENCE HOUSE

The year 2019 sees the 500th anniversary of the death of Leonardo da Vinci, surely one of the most fascinating figures of any age. To mark this momentous occasion, drawings by Leonardo from the incomparable holdings of the Royal Collection at Windsor Castle will be shown across the United Kingdom. In the Spring of 2019, selections of the finest of Leonardo's drawings will be shown simultaneously at twelve museums and galleries across England, Scotland, Wales and Northern Ireland. The Queen's Gallery at Buckingham Palace will show 200 drawings during the Summer – the largest exhibition of Leonardo's work in almost 70 years – and many of those drawings will be displayed at the Palace of Holyroodhouse in Edinburgh the following Winter. Together, these fourteen exhibitions will give an unprecedented opportunity for people throughout the nation to engage at first hand with the genius of Leonardo.

These drawings cover the whole range of Leonardo's artistic and scientific investigations and provide a remarkable insight into his world. Of Leonardo, perhaps more than of any other artist, it can truthfully be said that 'all human life is there': he used drawing to record, to explore and to think, and through this selection we can comprehend the many aspects of his boundless intelligence. From his studies of the human form – including his groundbreaking anatomical work – to his meditations on the beauty of Nature, and finally to his haunted visions of the end of the world, every variety of experience is laid before us – and that is perhaps why Leonardo still speaks so strongly to us today.

One of the principal aims of the Royal Collection Trust, of which I am Chairman, is that works of art from the Royal Collection should be seen and enjoyed as widely as possible, and I am delighted that these exhibitions will provide an unparalleled means of fulfilling that aim on behalf of Her Majesty The Queen. I am sure that everyone who visits these exhibitions will be as inspired as I have always been by Leonardo's brilliance.

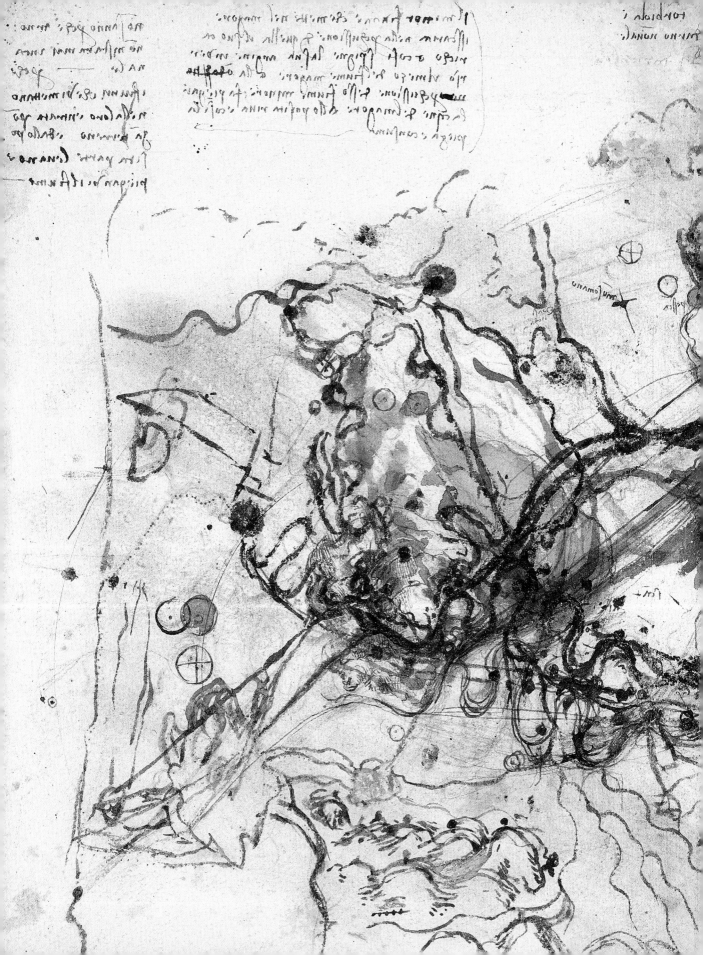

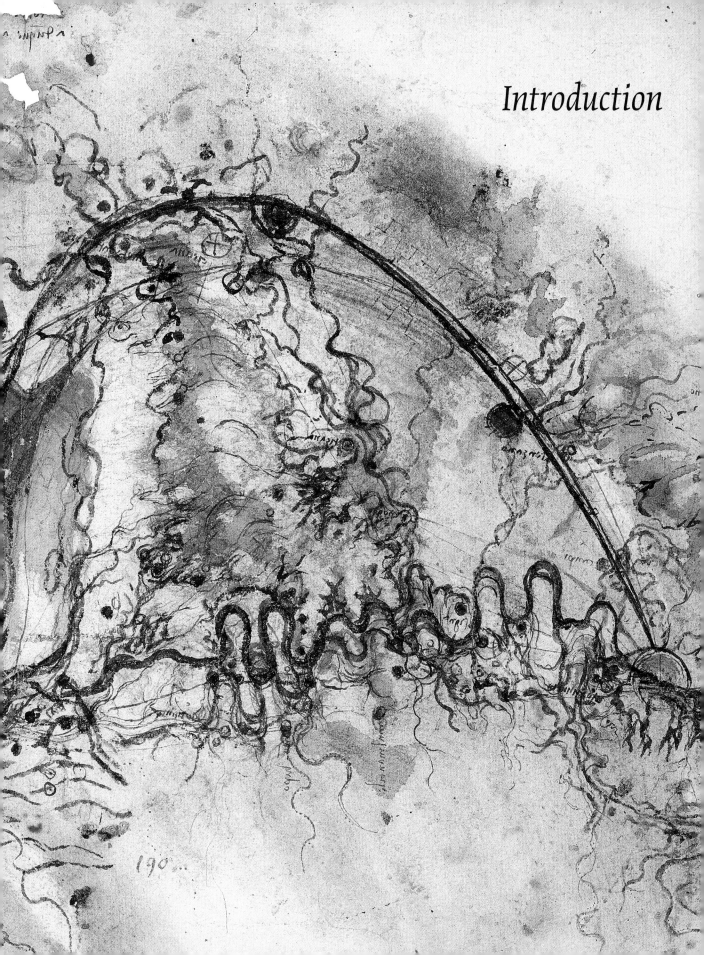

Introduction

LEONARDO DA VINCI was the archetypal 'Renaissance man', accomplished in painting, sculpture, architecture, music, anatomy, engineering, cartography, geology and botany. Yet the full extent of his achievements was unknown to his contemporaries and successors. He executed only 20 or so paintings, scattered across Italy and beyond; two of his three greatest compositions were never completed, and though one (the *Battle of Anghiari*) was hugely influential in Florence, it was obliterated within 60 years. No sculpture by Leonardo is known today: what would have been his masterpiece, an equestrian monument to Francesco Sforza, fell victim to the turbulence of politics and warfare that was a constant shadow over his career. And Leonardo's sustained, often ground-breaking scientific work, conducted with the aim of compiling treatises on many branches of knowledge, remained almost entirely unrecognised until his surviving manuscripts were transcribed and published in the late nineteenth century.

It is primarily through Leonardo's drawings and writings that we can begin to understand the man and his achievements. The manuscripts – held in the Biblioteca

Ambrosiana in Milan, the Bibliothèque de l'Institut de France in Paris, and a few other libraries – are unique in their interplay of words and images as Leonardo's ideas unfold on the page. Many hundreds of Leonardo's individual drawings survive, more than any other major artist of the Renaissance, and among the most wide-ranging and technically brilliant of any period. Around 600 have been kept together as a group since Leonardo's death in 1519, and have been in the Royal Collection since the seventeenth century. The finest of those drawings are presented here.

Only a small proportion of Leonardo's drawings are connected directly with his artistic projects. The remainder were his attempt to understand the infinite variety of experience, the theme of his whole career; while he developed a rich and powerful literary style, he always maintained that an image conveyed knowledge more accurately and concisely than any words. Few of his surviving drawings were intended for others to see: they are his private laboratory, for Leonardo used his drawings to think on paper – to devise new compositions, to fix fleeting impressions, to force himself to look in minute detail, to test his understanding, to explore every possible variant of a scenario. As will become clear, Leonardo's drawings allow us to enter one of the greatest minds in history, with a directness that no other medium allows.

Leonardo's life

Leonardo was born on 15 April 1452 near the town of Vinci, 15 miles (25 km) west of Florence in the Arno valley. He was the illegitimate son of a legal notary, Ser Piero da Vinci, and a peasant girl named Caterina, and was taken into his paternal grandfather's house in Vinci. We have no knowledge of Leonardo's education: he learned to read and write, but his arithmetical skills were always shaky, and though he tried to learn some Latin later in life, he never became comfortable with the language of most scientific writings.

On the death of his grandfather in 1464, the 12-year-old Leonardo may have moved to his father's household in Florence, but there is no record of his presence in the city until 1472, when he was registered as a member of the painters' confraternity, the Company of St Luke. From the following year we have the first certain work by Leonardo, a remarkable landscape drawing (fig. 1) inscribed with the date 5 August 1473. That inscription is in mirror-image, and to the end of his life Leonardo wrote his personal notes in this manner, from right to left. This was not an attempt to keep his researches secret, as has been claimed, for Leonardo's neat script is relatively easy to read with a little practice. Leonardo was left-handed, and mirror-writing may simply have been easier for him, pulling rather than pushing the pen against the nap of the paper, and avoiding smudging the ink with his hand.

At that time Leonardo was probably working in the studio of the great sculptor and painter Andrea del Verrocchio (3) in Florence, though it is not certain that Verrocchio had been Leonardo's principal teacher, and he is documented in Verrocchio's studio

FIG.1
A landscape in the Arno valley, 1473.
Pen and ink. 19.4 × 28.5 cm.
Florence, Uffizi

only in 1476 (when he was accused of sodomy, charges that were dismissed). During the mid-1470s Leonardo executed paintings independently while still putting his hand to products of Verrocchio's studio – his *Annunciation* (Florence, Uffizi) and portrait of Ginevra de' Benci (Washington, D.C., National Gallery of Art), entirely by Leonardo, are earlier in style than his contribution to the *Baptism of Christ* (Uffizi), a collaborative work of Verrocchio's studio.

In January 1478 Leonardo was commissioned to paint an altarpiece for a chapel in the seat of government in Florence, the Palazzo della Signoria. He seems not to have fulfilled this commission, instead beginning work in 1480 or 1481 on a painting of the *Adoration of the Magi* for the church of San Donato a Scopeto outside Florence, for which his father was the notary. In September 1481 Leonardo took delivery of a barrel of wine as part payment for this work, but the painting remained unfinished (fig. 4), and nothing is known of his life for the next 18 months.

By April 1483 Leonardo had settled in Milan, where he received the commission for an altarpiece known as the *Virgin of the Rocks* (see **20**), and he was to remain in the city for the next 16 years. Leonardo's reasons for moving from Florence to Milan are unclear: one early biographer stated that he was sent by the de facto ruler of Florence, Lorenzo de' Medici, to present a silver lyre in the shape of a horse's head to Ludovico Sforza, later Duke of Milan. In the mid-1480s Leonardo entered Ludovico's service, initially to work on an equestrian monument to Ludovico's father (**40–48**), but in time requiring him to take on a wide range of tasks – portraits (**16–17**), designs for architecture and entertainments (**49–55, 57**) and, after work on the equestrian monument had ground to a halt around 1494, his greatest finished painting, the *Last Supper* (**56–61**).

Leonardo's years in Milan also saw the expansion of his interests into military, scientific and theoretical matters (**21–33**). A deep interest in the representation of light and shade, perspective, atmospheric recession, the posing of figures, the depiction of drapery, water, trees and so on was already latent in Leonardo's paintings, and from a combination of received wisdom and personal experience he started to prepare a treatise on painting – on the theoretical basis of depicting the world, rather than technical know-how. He assembled a small library, and for the rest of his life he gathered material towards the treatise. But it proved impossible to limit its scope: within a few years Leonardo had started to plan a separate treatise on the human body (**34–39** and **119–143**), and as his aim was ultimately to understand every aspect of the visible world, in time he compiled material towards treatises on water, mechanics, the growth of plants and many other subjects, none of which was ever finished.

During his time in Milan, Leonardo rose from being a mere painter – just a craftsman – to the position of court artist at the heart of one of the most powerful states in Italy. But that power was always vulnerable to superior force, and in late 1499 a French army invaded Lombardy and overthrew Ludovico Sforza. Leonardo lost his patron and his position, but before he left Milan he acquired French patrons and commissions that were to be of importance to the end of his life.

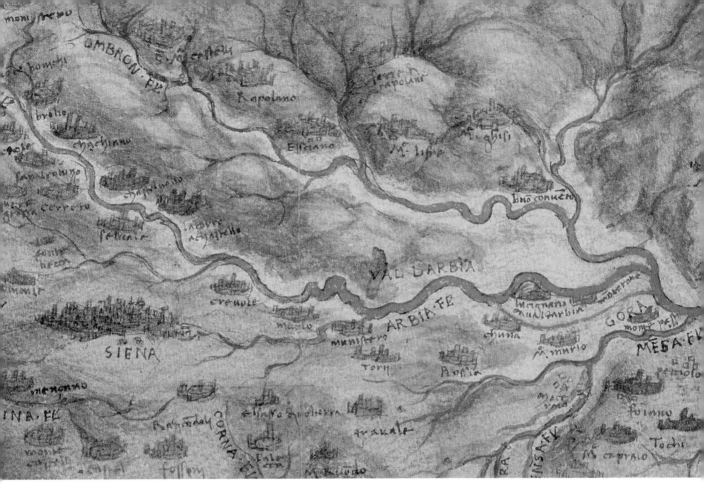

Detail of **89**

After travelling briefly to Venice (and possibly to Rome and Naples), Leonardo returned to Florence in 1500. His first works back in the city of his youth were the *Madonna of the Yarnwinder* (**64**) and a cartoon of the *Madonna and Child with St Anne and a lamb* (**154–159**); but Leonardo was reported to be preoccupied with geometry, painting little and 'very impatient with the brush'. In the summer of 1502, at the age of 50, he therefore took a position as military architect and engineer to Cesare Borgia, son of Pope Alexander VI and commander of the papal army. For the remainder of 1502 Leonardo toured Cesare's newly conquered territories to the east of Florence, visiting Cesena, Rimini, Urbino, Pesaro and Imola (**84**), surveying the fortifications and rekindling his earlier interest in military theory (**85**).

Leonardo remained with Cesare for only a few months, and by March 1503 he was back in Florence. He began work on the *Mona Lisa* (fig. 17) and *Leda and the Swan* (**66– 68**), and continued to make maps, now for the Florentine government – surveying the area around Pisa (see **87**), the Valdichiana (**88–89**), and the Arno to the east and west of Florence (**90–93**). His principal project was the painting of a huge mural, the *Battle of Anghiari*, in the council chamber of the Palazzo della Signoria (**71–83**), the most prestigious commission of Leonardo's career. But in the summer of 1506 Leonardo obtained leave to return to Milan at the request of the French occupiers, marking the start of an unsettled two years during which he travelled repeatedly between Florence and Milan. The *Battle of Anghiari* fell into abeyance and was never finished;

Detail of **101**

instead, Leonardo occupied himself with intermittent work on easel paintings and an immersion in scientific study, particularly human anatomy. In the winter of 1507–8 he dissected an old man in the hospital of Santa Maria Nuova in Florence, and the resulting drawings (**119–120**) were to be the basis of his greatest achievements in anatomy, after his decisive return to Milan in the spring of 1508 (**124–143**).

Leonardo lived in and around Milan for the next five years. He probably began work on the painting of the *Madonna and Child with St Anne and a lamb* (**154–159**) during this period; he dissected more corpses in the medical school of the University of Pavia (**125–136**); he planned a villa for the governor of Milan (**147**) and designed another equestrian monument, to the mercenary commander Gian Giacomo Trivulzio (**149–151**). But once again military strife disrupted Leonardo's work. By 1511 the French occupiers of Milan were under increasing pressure from a 'Holy League' of papal, Venetian and Spanish forces, and in 1512 Swiss forces supported by both the Pope and the Holy Roman Emperor occupied a part of Milan, installing as Duke the son of Ludovico Sforza (who had died in French captivity in 1508). Massimiliano Sforza was in no position to resume the artistic patronage of his father, and, as Leonardo had now lost his French employers too, he spent much time at the family villa of his well-born assistant Francesco Melzi, at Vaprio to the east of Milan. There he designed improvements to the villa (**152** and the reverse of **118**) and continued to pursue his scientific studies, primarily his anatomical investigations, with dogs, birds and oxen (**137–143**) as his subjects.

Leonardo finally abandoned Lombardy in September 1513 and travelled to Rome, where he was based for the next three years under the patronage of Giuliano de' Medici, brother of the recently elected Pope Leo X. The Vatican had become the centre of the High Renaissance, with Michelangelo's Sistine Chapel ceiling newly unveiled and Raphael at work in the Stanze. But Leonardo's artistic activities in the city are obscure, and he made frequent trips away from Rome, to Civitavecchia and Parma in 1514, and to Florence, Bologna and possibly the Pontine Marshes (**95**) in 1515.

Giuliano de' Medici died in March 1516, and our last record of Leonardo's presence in Rome is in August 1516, when he was surveying the basilica of San Paolo fuori le mura. By January 1517 he was in the Loire valley in central France, at the court of the young King Francis I. The French had been aware of Leonardo's talents since their occupation of Milan in 1499: his works had been sought by a succession of French patrons, and Leonardo's inventiveness had been brought directly to the attention of Francis I by his design of a mechanical lion, commissioned by the Florentine community in Lyon to welcome the newly crowned King into that city in July 1515.

Leonardo, now aged 64, settled at Amboise, one of a chain of royal residences in the Loire valley, where he held a privileged position as painter, engineer and architect to the King. During his last years Leonardo painted little, though he and his assistants were still working on the *St Anne* and *Mona Lisa*. Designs for a few other artistic and architectural projects can be dated to these years, including another equestrian monument (**179–186**), but Leonardo mostly earned his keep by advising on technical matters, by providing designs for entertainments (**170–176**), and generally by being an adornment to the court. Some years later, the sculptor Benvenuto Cellini reported Francis I as saying that he 'took such pleasure in hearing [Leonardo] talk that he would only on a few days of the year deprive himself of his company'.[1] After what may have been two of the most gratifying years of his life, Leonardo died at Amboise on 2 May 1519.

Leonardo's drawing materials

Leonardo's early drawings were little different from those of his contemporaries – compositional sketches (**4**), studies of details for paintings (**6–10**), and drawing exercises (**13–14**), executed in metalpoint or pen and ink. Pens were cut from goose quills, and the ink was made by mixing iron salts with tannic acid from oak galls. Metalpoint involves drawing with a stylus, usually of silver, on paper coated with a preparation of finely ground bone, often with pigment added (e.g. **7–8**, **13**). The stylus leaves a grey trace of the metal on the slightly abrasive ground; varying the pressure on the stylus does not change the character of the line, and the mark cannot be erased. Metalpoint demands control and discipline, and was the standard medium for training young artists in fifteenth-century Italy, though it largely fell into disuse after 1500. Leonardo tended to use metalpoint for drawings from the life, and the looser medium of pen and ink for sketches from the imagination.

In the early 1490s Leonardo began to draw with natural red and black chalks (a red-ochre variety of haematite and a soft carbonaceous schist respectively). They soon supplanted metalpoint in his drawings, and from then onwards he was to use chalks in every manner conceivable: for rapid sketches (**57**), heavily worked compositional studies (**65**), intricately modelled drawings using the point of the chalk (**96**) and smoky studies of form (**104**). Leonardo used toned washes or coloured grounds for some of his chalk drawings, most frequently an orange-red ground for red chalk drawings (**59–60**, **106–110**), thereby restricting the available tonal range to allow the most subtle modelling.

The years around 1510 were marked by an increasingly experimental manipulation of all available media, layering black, red and occasionally white chalks with liquid media on a red ground, to give a richness to studies of hair, drapery and atmospheric landscapes (**100**, **157**, **160**). In his last years Leonardo purged his drawings of much of their former colour, eliminating red chalk and restricting his materials to black chalk, pen and ink, and wash, even in a few drawings working in black chalk on a dark grey ground (**199**).

All Leonardo's drawings are executed on paper (usually white, but occasionally blue), made from clothing rags of hemp or linen. The book-printing revolution of the fifteenth century had led to an expansion in the manufacture of paper throughout Europe: its price was falling relative to that of parchment, and during Leonardo's lifetime paper became an everyday commodity, encouraging artists to use it more freely and experimentally. But Leonardo's drawings were never trifles to be thrown away, and he hoarded dozens of notebooks and thousands of loose sheets to the end of his life, bequeathing them to his faithful assistant Francesco Melzi (see **1–2**). The subsequent efforts of two obsessive collectors, Pompeo Leoni and Thomas Howard; the strength and stability of Leonardo's materials; and good fortune, in the avoidance of flood, fire and simple loss – all these factors have ensured that many of Leonardo's drawings have survived the last 500 years in excellent condition, and that they can be seen much as Leonardo drew them.

Detail of **36**

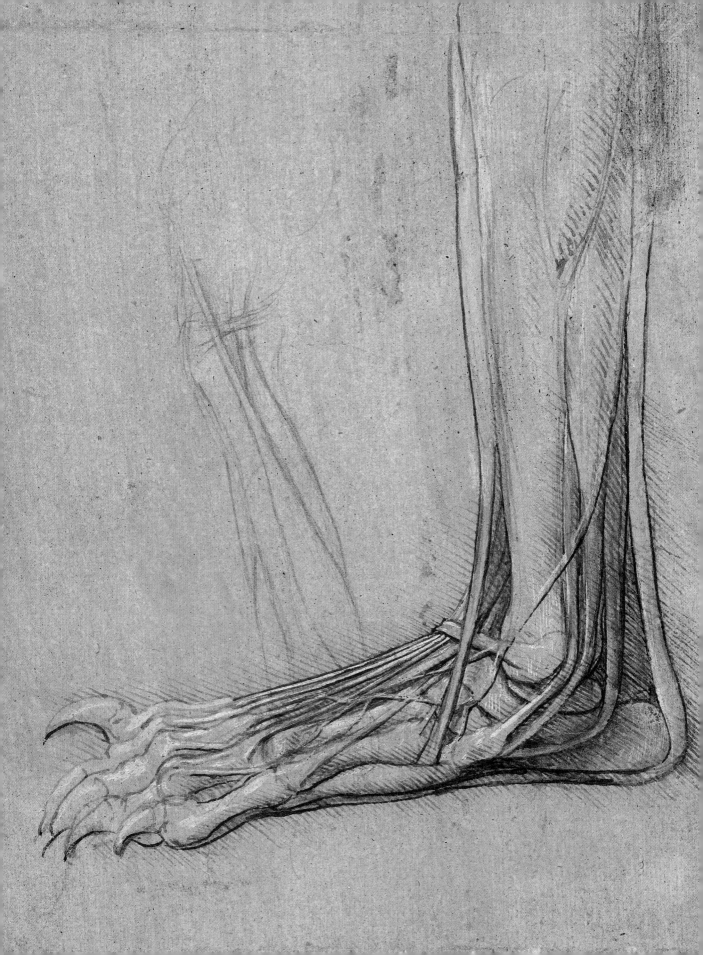

Notes on the catalogue

It is difficult to trace a continuous narrative in
Leonardo's career, for his work is characterised by a
multitude of simultaneous pursuits – artistic projects
that stretched on for years or even decades, and
scientific interests that evolved and cross-fertilised
from the 1480s onwards. While this book is generally
organised chronologically, individual works are grouped
thematically, with sections on Leonardo's map-making,
landscapes, botany, anatomy, water studies and so on.

All works are by Leonardo unless otherwise stated,
and all are on white paper unless a colour or coating
is specified. Many drawings are irregularly cut, and
maximum dimensions are given, height before width.
The numbers added by Francesco Melzi in the sixteenth
century (see **2**) and a few other early inscriptions are
transcribed, but the mark of Edward VII (1901–10)
stamped in the lower right corner of many drawings is
not mentioned. The Royal Collection Inventory Number
(RCIN) can be used to access high-resolution images
of all Leonardo's drawings in the Royal Collection at
www.rct.uk

THE DRAWINGS

The Portrait of Leonardo and the Leoni binding

1

Attributed to Francesco Melzi (1491/3–c.1570)

A portrait of Leonardo, c.1515–18

Red chalk. 27.5 × 19.0 cm. RCIN 912726

Although not by Leonardo, this drawing is of high quality and is the most objective and accurate portrait of the master to survive. Only one other drawing may with some confidence be taken as a true likeness of Leonardo, a sketch by a pupil on a late sheet of studies showing the artist at about the same age (166).

All early writers were agreed that Leonardo was beautiful – even if none had known him personally – and that this was a natural, god-given corollary of his personal qualities and his abilities as an artist. The increasingly explicit concept during the sixteenth century of the individual as a mutable social construct required authors to attribute grace and elegance to Leonardo, as a necessary condition for the newly elevated social position for the artist: the artisan of a century earlier was now expected to cultivate the ease of deportment and nobility of Castiglione's ideal courtier.

Of the early authors, only the appendix to a brief biography by the so-called Anonimo Gaddiano gives some detail of Leonardo's appearance, describing him as having 'a beautiful head of hair down to the middle of his breast, in ringlets and well arranged'.[2] There is however no evidence that Leonardo was bearded until his last years. Before the sixteenth century a beard would have been seen as odd on an Italian: they were the preserve of the barbarous, Germans, orientals, figures from ancient history, mythology and Biblical times, philosophers, hermits, and penitents. Pope Julius II grew a beard in 1510 in penitence for the French invasion of Italy, but it seems to have been King Francis I who from his accession in 1515 sparked the pan-European fashion for beards that endured throughout the sixteenth century.

The present portrait was most probably executed from the life by Leonardo's pupil Francesco Melzi, though the chalk is more richly handled and varied in its textures than in the copy drawings usually attributed to Melzi; there may even be some enlivening strokes by Leonardo himself in the lower part of the hair. Unusually for a drawing from the Melzi/Leoni collection, the sheet has been shaped for mounting, the paper has discoloured from exposure to light, and the sheet shows signs of having been attached to a support, lifted and restored at an early date. It was presumably framed and hung as a memento of the master, and may well have been the portrait seen by Vasari in Melzi's villa many years later: 'Francesco cherishes and preserves these papers as relics of Leonardo, together with the portrait of that artist of such happy memory.'[3]

It was possibly through Vasari's acquaintance with this drawing in the Villa Melzi that the profile frontispiece to the biography of Leonardo in his *Lives of the Artists* (1568) took the form that it did; and from Vasari's illustration stemmed posterity's image of Leonardo. Intriguingly, the standard type of Aristotle converged with this likeness of Leonardo during the sixteenth century, to become the accepted pattern for the venerable natural philosopher. This fitted so perfectly the standard perception of Leonardo's character before the twentieth century that a now-famous drawing at Turin was unquestioningly accepted as a self-portrait of Leonardo when it surfaced in the early nineteenth century. That old man with furrowed brow and long beard, gazing into the distance, soon passed into common currency as the definitive likeness of Leonardo and will doubtless retain this status. Only recently has it been pointed out that the drawing is in fact a work of the 1490s, when Leonardo was in his mid-forties, and cannot possibly be a self-portrait.

2

The Leoni binding, c.1590

Leather, gold tooling. 47.0 × 33.0 × 6.5 cm.
RCIN 933320

On Leonardo's death in France on 2 May 1519, he bequeathed to his pupil Francesco Melzi 'each and every one of his books' and 'other tools and depictions [*Instrumenti et Portracti*] pertaining to his art and craft of painting', presumably including his drawings.[4] Melzi took this mass of material back to his family residence at Vaprio outside Milan, and over the next 50 years attempted to put Leonardo's papers into order, arranging the loose sheets broadly by subject matter in at least five sequences which he annotated with consecutive numbers, seen on most of the drawings here.

After Melzi's death around 1570, the sculptor Pompeo Leoni acquired the bulk of the loose sheets from Melzi's son, and mounted them on the pages of (at least) two albums: technical studies in the large Codex Atlanticus, now in the Biblioteca Ambrosiana in Milan, and more artistic drawings in a smaller album, containing around 600 sheets mounted on 234 folios. That album was listed in an inventory of Leoni's residence after his death in Madrid in 1608, and by 1630 it was in England, in the collection of Thomas Howard, 14th Earl of Arundel, then the greatest collector of drawings in Europe. The album may have been a direct purchase by one of Arundel's agents; alternatively, it may have been acquired by the Prince of Wales (later Charles I) during his visit to Madrid in 1623, or by his companion on that trip, the Duke of Buckingham, and acquired by Arundel soon after.

On the outbreak of the Civil War in 1642, Arundel left England for Antwerp, taking some, but not all, of his collection with him. Henry Howard, grandson of the Earl and later 6th Duke of Norfolk, was noted as being

in possession of part of Arundel's collection in 1655, and in 1663/4 he was displaying to Christmas guests at the family palace in Norwich 'prints and draughts done by most of the Great Masters own hands … most of them collected by the old Earl of Arundel who employed his agents in most places to buy him up rarities'.[5]

By 1690 the Leonardo album was in royal ownership, for Constantijn Huygens, secretary to William III, noted in his diary that at Whitehall Palace 'we looked through four or five books of drawings, including some by Holbein and Leonardo da Vinci'. It is probable that the album had passed to the royal collection some years earlier – most likely Henry Howard gave it (and another of drawings by Hans Holbein) to Charles II, perhaps in thanks for the restitution of the Norfolk lands and titles after the Restoration of the monarchy in 1660.

Over the next century and a half the album received little attention, moving between various royal residences until it finally settled in the new Royal Library at Windsor Castle in the 1830s. During the reign of Queen Victoria the drawings were removed from the albums and mounted individually, allowing them to be exhibited; by the early twentieth century all the Leonardos had been mounted, and many were then stamped in the lower right corner with the cipher of Edward VII. Whereas most bindings were discarded during this process, the Leoni binding was fortunately preserved as a relic of the master, the repository for three centuries of much of what we know about Leonardo.

DISEGNI·DI·LEONARDO·

·DA·VINCI·RESTAV

RATI·

·DA·POMPEO·

·LEONI·

FIG.2
Andrea del Verrocchio and studio,
The Madonna and Child with angels
(detail), *c.*1476–8.
Tempera on panel. 96.5 × 70.7 cm.
London, National Gallery

3

Attributed to Andrea del Verrocchio (*c.*1435–1488)

*A lily, c.*1475

Stylus, pinpointing, leadpoint, pen and ink,
brown wash, ochre wash and rubbing, white
heightening (partly discoloured), pricked through.
31.4 × 17.7 cm. Melzi's *199*. RCIN 912418

The drawing depicts a lily (*Lilium candidum* L.), a symbol
of purity in depictions of the Virgin. The technique is
unusually elaborate, and the outlines of the lower part
of the lily were pricked through with a needle, to transfer
the design to another support by pouncing charcoal dust
through the holes. The upper part of the flower was probably drawn after the pricking, for the unpricked stem does
not join convincingly to the central branching. In the lower
part of the sheet is an unrelated perspectival construction.

Although the drawing formed part of the Leonardo
group inherited by Francesco Melzi, it is unlike any other
sheet in style and technique. The thick, deliberate pen
line bears close comparison to several of the few known
drawings by Leonardo's early associate and probable
master, Andrea del Verrocchio, and the sophisticated
spatial presentation of the lily echoes Verrocchio's
mature style; the lily is close in character (if not in detail)
to that in his *Madonna* in the National Gallery (fig. 2).
While the mechanical nature of pricking was uncongenial
to Leonardo and used only rarely by him (**87**, **123**), it is
often found in Verrocchio's sheets. An attribution to
the older artist therefore seems plausible: Leonardo
presumably came by the sheet while in Verrocchio's
workshop, and it must have been both an inspiration
and a challenge when he was to make his own acutely
observed flower drawings 30 years later (**105–112**).

4
The Madonna and Child with the infant Baptist, and heads in profile, c.1478–80

Pen and ink. 40.5 × 29.0 cm. RCIN 912276
(Detail shown pp. 24–5)

A large sketch of the *Madonna and Child with the infant Baptist* fills almost the whole page. The Madonna is our first sight of the kneeling figure that Leonardo returned to repeatedly during his career (**66**); her head is in two positions, looking tenderly at the twisting, suckling Child, and gazing sombrely downwards towards us, while a few lines indicate a watery landscape with precipitous hills, as seen in many of Leonardo's paintings. No corresponding painting by Leonardo is known, but several variants by followers may indicate that he worked it up at least as far as a cartoon.

Leonardo then filled every remaining space with 13 impassive human profiles (and another 11 on the reverse of the sheet), two roaring lions and a snarling dragon. He is exploring how small variations can change a beautiful youth into a child, a young woman or an old man. These were standard Florentine types but struck a deep chord in Leonardo, and remained a constant in his work – seen in doodles, comic grotesques (**49**, **52**), studies for paintings such as the *Last Supper* (**57–60**), and finished drawings with no apparent function (**160–165**).

5
Studies of dragons, c.1478–80

Stylus, leadpoint, pen and ink.
15.9 × 24.3 cm. Melzi's 52. RCIN 912370

In his first Florentine period Leonardo often sketched a horseman fighting a dragon, a concept that became entangled in his mind with the horses for the *Adorations* (**6–10**). Here he studies a dragon reeling away from the impact of a lance; an almost invisible stylus sketch at upper left shows (with the sheet inverted) the dragon slumped in defeat.

The dragons conform to the standard Renaissance advice to create a monster by assembling the parts of different animals, as Leonardo himself recommended:

If you wish to make an animal imagined by you appear natural, let us say a dragon, take for its head that of a mastiff or hound, with the eyes of a cat, the ears of a porcupine, the nose of a greyhound, the brow of a lion, the temples of an old cock, and the neck of a terrapin.[6]

Here the wings are half-bird, half-bat, the legs are a lion's, the head a dog's, the neck and tail like a snake; but the body resembles a plucked chicken, and Leonardo was remarkably uncertain in attaching the different parts to this torso – it is hard to distinguish front from back, or how the beast might look when not under attack.

Detail of **7**

The *Adoration of the Shepherds* and the *Adoration of the Magi*

Leonardo's first substantial group of drawings to survive
are studies towards a composition of the *Adoration of
the Shepherds* – the Madonna kneeling in adoration
over the infant Christ (fig. 3), surrounded by figures,
horses, oxen and asses. They may have been made for
a commission he received in January 1478, an altarpiece
(of unspecified subject) for the chapel of San Bernardo
in the Palazzo della Signoria, Florence. That commission
was apparently not fulfilled by Leonardo; instead, by
March 1481 at the latest (and possibly a year earlier),
he began an ambitious painting of the *Adoration of the
Magi*, for the church of San Donato a Scopeto outside
Florence. The last recorded payment to Leonardo was
made in September 1481, and probably soon afterwards
he left Florence, abandoning the panel as an underpainting (fig. 4). Inevitably, Leonardo's sketches for the
Shepherds informed his ideas for the *Magi*, though there
is a clear transition from the bucolic, gently devout
earlier drawings to the more agitated studies for the
Magi, and the underpainting has an otherworldly
aspect unprecedented in Florentine art.

FIG. 3 [ABOVE]
The Adoration of the Shepherds, c.1478–80.
Leadpoint, pen and ink. 21.3 × 15.2 cm.
Bayonne, musée Bonnat-Helleu

FIG. 4
The Adoration of the Magi, c.1481.
Oil and tempera on panel. 243 × 246 cm.
Florence, Uffizi

6
Studies of horses, c.1478–80

Leadpoint, pen and ink. 10.7 × 18.3 cm.
Melzi's 35. RCIN 912324

7
Studies of horses, and a horse and lanceman, c.1478–80

Metalpoint, pen and ink, on orange
prepared paper. 11.7 × 19.4 cm.
Melzi's 108. RCIN 912325
(Detail shown p. 29)

All the related studies at Windsor are of animals, perhaps retained by Leonardo for future reference: even at this early stage of his career, his approach was to make a range of studies of relevant subject matter in addition to compositional sketches. The first four drawings here are for the earlier *Adoration of the Shepherds*. The studies in **6**, show a horse from three directions – the hind leg from the left, the whole horse from the right, and the bony rear of the animal from behind. Both the horse and the draughtsmanship are delicate and slightly nervous, a common trait of Leonardo's earliest studies.

A similar horse is seen in **7**, with long tufts of hair at the fetlocks, though the casual pose of **6** is replaced at lower left here by a formal pacing gait, both right legs advanced. At upper left are two more dynamic poses, in metalpoint only – a rearing horse with its rider thrusting a lance (possibly related to the dragons in **5**); and the outlines of a horse struggling to regain its feet, its head twisted backwards, the first appearance of what would become a favourite motif (**65**, **75**, **178**). The paper is coated with a bright orange preparation composed mainly of red lead.

The drawing illustrated in **8** shows horses grazing: one directly from behind, as in **6** but now with its head visible to the left of its legs, and another from in front, its head obscured by the first. To the left a horse is drawn in profile, though only the right legs are inked, and the faint metalpoint of the rest of the animal is almost invisible against the brown-grey preparation, coloured with red lead mixed with ground charcoal.

8
Studies of horses, c.1478–80
Metalpoint, pen and ink, touches of red
chalk, on brown-grey prepared paper.
14.3 × 19.6 cm. Melzi's *100*. RCIN 912308

9
An ox and ass, and other studies of asses, c.1478–80
Leadpoint, pen and ink. 16.4 × 17.7 cm.
Melzi's *36*. RCIN 912362

10
Studies of horses, c.1480–81
Metalpoint on cream prepared paper.
11.4 × 19.6 cm. Melzi's *111*. RCIN 912315

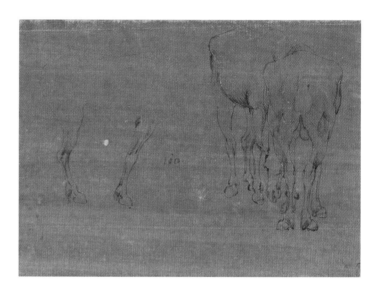

In **9** we see the ox and ass that in legend breathed
on the newborn Christ to keep him warm; the animals,
posed differently, are present in the right background
of fig. 4. Surrounding them here are studies in scratchy
leadpoint of a horse or ass, its head down as if to graze;
at upper left the bending rider twists his head to gaze
upwards, perhaps at the Star of Bethlehem. The stains
of burnt umber suggest that the sheet was in use in the
workshop while painting was taking place.

The hard, linear metalpoint of **6–9** is transformed in
10, which has a softness beyond anything previously seen
in Leonardo's drawings. The horse is more classically
built, with a muscular neck and flowing mane, and the
profile presentation suggests the inspiration of a Roman
relief, though no sculptural source available to Leonardo
in Florence has been identified. Horses rearing and
bucking are seen in the background of the *Adoration of
the Magi*, both the painting and a perspectival drawing
also in the Uffizi, and though none is in this profile
pose, the agitated, febrile atmosphere of the drawing
must connect it with the later of the two *Adorations*.

11

A horse with lines of proportion, c.1480

Leadpoint, pen and ink. 29.8 × 29.0 cm. RCIN 912318

The physical type of the horse is that of Leonardo's first Florentine period (cf. **6–7**), as is the style of the drawing, with rough outlines and patches of scribbled hatching. Leonardo seems to be investigating the principles of equine anatomy independently of any composition, but the absence of annotations suggests that he simply sketched a horse and drew lines between salient points, without measuring a live animal or attempting to determine any module of proportion.

In this drawing Leonardo may have been emulating his former associate Andrea del Verrocchio, whose last great work was the bronze equestrian monument of

Bartolomeo Colleoni (Venice, Campo Santi Giovanni e Paolo), commissioned in the early 1480s on the basis of a model. A drawing by Verrocchio (New York, Metropolitan Museum) depicts a horse standing in left profile with lines drawn over the body, as here, but with measurements written by each line. Verrocchio had reportedly been in competition with two other artists for the commission, and Leonardo has occasionally been suggested as one of his rivals; it is thus conceivable, if unlikely, that this drawing was preparatory for a competition model by Leonardo for the Colleoni project.

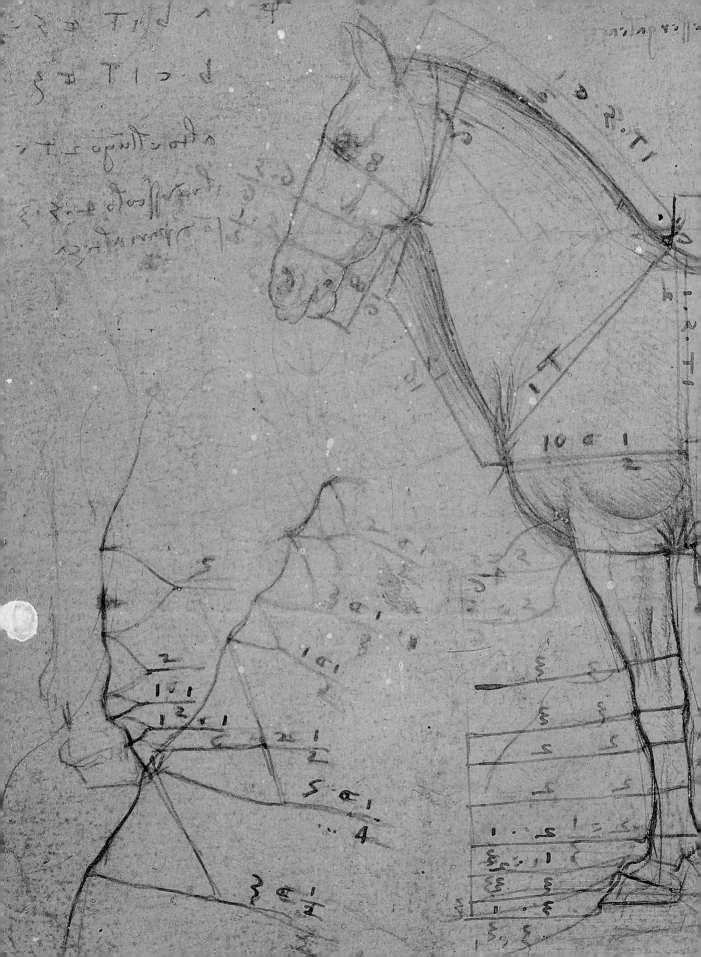

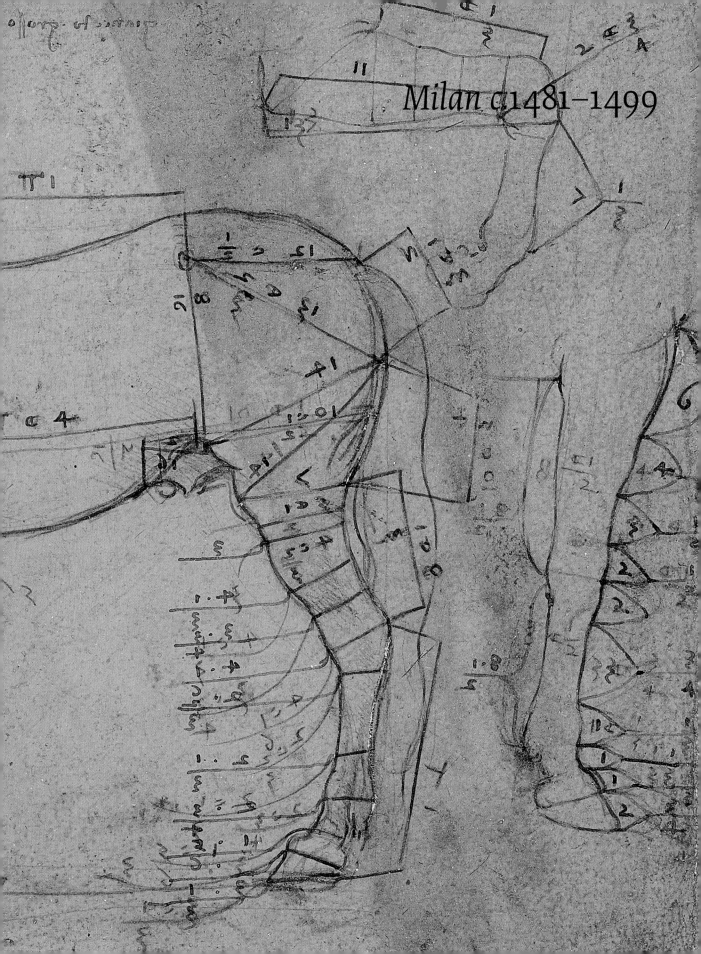

Milan c1481–1499

Earlier artistic drawings

12

A portrait of a man in profile,
c.1482–5

Metalpoint on cream prepared paper.
12.7 × 10.6 cm.
Melzi's 50. RCIN 912498

The metalpoint was probably always rather faint, for Leonardo strengthened the profile emphatically, detracting from the delicate modelling and the quality of light in the eyes. His wish to fix the profile at the expense of the pictorial effect suggests that the drawing was preparatory for some other work, presumably a small (and rather conventional) painting – Leonardo may well have been responsible for more than his three known Milanese portraits. The profile resembles the known likenesses of Galeazzo Maria Sforza, the former Duke of Milan, but he had been assassinated in 1476; a large nose was however a distinctive trait of the Sforza, and the sitter may have been another member of that family.

13

A nude youth as
St John the Baptist, c.1485

Metalpoint, white heightening, on
blue-grey prepared paper. 17.8 × 12.2 cm.
Melzi's 68. RCIN 912572

FIG.5
Marco d'Oggiono, *St Sebastian, c.1490.*
Oil on panel. 60.9 × 28.1 cm.
Milan, Museo Poldi Pezzoli

It is hard to get a clear picture of Leonardo's development
as a painter during the 1480s. Between the documented
first version of the *Virgin of the Rocks* (1483–*c.*1485; Paris,
Louvre) and the portrait of Cecilia Gallerani (*c.*1490; fig. 6)
we have only the *Portrait of a Musician* (Milan, Ambrosiana)
and the unfinished *St Jerome* (Vatican, Pinacoteca), both
of uncertain date – a meagre output from almost a
decade's work. But Leonardo was making great strides
as an artist, aiming at a balance and fullness of form that
was to culminate in the *Last Supper* of the 1490s (fig. 11).

This progress would have been achieved through
studio practice as much as through commissioned works.

14
Two studies of a standing male nude, c.1490

Metalpoint, white heightening, on blue-grey prepared paper.
17.7 × 14.0 cm. RCIN 912637

The two drawings here are the sort of exercise that would have been obligatory for any ambitious artist in the Renaissance – figure studies from posed models to hone the artist's draughtsmanship, observational skills and knowledge of human form, and to encourage the development of a personal style (or allow an assistant to learn his master's style). **13** is a study of a languid youth posed as St John the Baptist, holding a reed cross that is shown again in the right margin; the distinctive arrangement of the legs is reproduced in a painting of *St Sebastian* by a follower of Leonardo (fig. 5), a subject that Leonardo himself sketched repeatedly in the 1480s.

The style of the metalpoint dates the work to the mid-1480s (cf. **40**), with highlights in white lead applied with a fine brush. The elegance and elongated proportions of Florentine art clearly persisted in Leonardo's work after he moved to Milan.

The form of the body in **14** is more robust: there is still an element of idealisation, but it is now a classical ideal. Leonardo was interested in how the fall of light reveals the muscles beneath the skin, and in the twisting and tilting of the torso caused by the model bearing his weight mainly on one leg (in Italian *contrapposto*).

15
A portrait of a woman in profile, c.1485–90

Metalpoint on cream prepared paper. 32.0 × 20.0 cm.
Melzi's *14*. RCIN 912505. (Detail shown p. 36)

Leonardo executed at least five portrait paintings
during his career, of which the most famous, the
Mona Lisa (fig. 17), is the least typical, for the sitter is
so idealised that she has lost her individuality. This
beautiful drawing is wholly different, a rigorously
observed study of a young woman in everyday clothing,
probably drawn not as a preparation for a painting
but as a finished work for Leonardo's own satisfaction.
The handling of the metalpoint ranges from sweeping
outlines in the bust and flowing locks of loose hair to
restrained modelling in the face – the cheek is hardly
touched, but small patches of shading at the eye,
nose and chin are so sensitively modulated that they
articulate the entire form; even the moistness of the
eye and its refracted light are conveyed. Leonardo had
attained complete mastery of this inflexible drawing
tool, using line alone to capture the most subtle effects.

16 [OPPOSITE]
Sketches of a woman, bust length, c.1490

Metalpoint on pale pinkish-buff prepared paper.
23.2 × 19.0 cm. Melzi's *49*. RCIN 912513

Leonardo drew his model 18 times in two basic
positions, from the front with her bust turned to the
left, and from behind looking over her left shoulder.
One can reconstruct the order in which Leonardo
filled his page, and what may be the last sketch, in the
centre of the left edge, is in the pose of Leonardo's
portrait of a *Lady with an Ermine* (fig. 6), almost certainly
depicting Cecilia Gallerani, and painted while she was
the mistress of Ludovico Sforza between 1489 and early
1491. This date would accord well with the confident
style of the drawing. The pose of Cecilia in the painting
is unconventional: she and her ermine are caught in a
momentary reaction to an event beyond the picture
frame, and that sense of spontaneity is what Leonardo
was searching for here. The model need not look like
Cecilia, as portraitists have commonly used a substitute
model in studying a pose, referring to the subject of
the portrait only for elements that required a likeness –
often no more than the face.

17

A study of a woman's hands, c.1490

Charcoal, metalpoint, white heightening,
on pale pinkish-buff prepared paper.
21.5 × 15.0 cm. Melzi's *210*. RCIN 912558

This is not a study of two hands held one above the
other, but two separate studies of crossed hands, each
study concentrating on one hand only, with the other
as a mere outline. The uppermost hand may be holding
something, perhaps a flower or a ring. The drawing
has often been connected with Leonardo's portrait
of Ginevra de' Benci of the mid-1470s (Washington,
D.C., National Gallery of Art), which is cut down and
probably once included the sitter's hands. The style
of the drawing is however significantly later than
that painting, with a combination of strong searching
outlines and rapid but controlled parallel hatching,
characteristic of Leonardo's metalpoint drawings of
around 1490 (cf. **42–43**).

Like **16**, this sheet may have been preparatory for
the portrait of Cecilia Gallerani (fig. 6). It is likely that
Leonardo had been contemplating the prominent,
active role of her hands from the outset – two sketches
in **16** show the model with her left arm akimbo or her
arms folded. The hands here do not correspond in pose
with those in the painting, but they are identical in
type, slender and elegant, and it is quite possible that
the drawing was an early study for the portrait, before
the decision was taken to introduce the ermine.

FIG.6
A Lady with an Ermine (Cecilia Gallerani),
*c.*1490. Oil on panel. 54.8 × 40.3 cm.
National Museum in Kraków /
the Princes Czartoryski Museum

18

*Studies of an infant, c.*1490–92

Metalpoint, pen and ink, on pale pinkish-
buff prepared paper. 17.1 × 21.8 cm.
Melzi's 4 (verso). RCIN 912569

19 [OPPOSITE]

*Studies of an infant, c.*1490–92

Red chalk. 13.8 × 19.5 cm. Melzi's 207.
RCIN 912568

The fluent lines of **18** suggest a date not long before Leonardo abandoned metalpoint in the early 1490s, while **19** is one of his earliest substantial red chalk drawings, the chalk handled in a linear manner with little awareness of its tonal possibilities. The sketches can be related to several of Leonardo's compositions of the *Madonna and Child* over a period of more than a decade. In both sheets the largest study is of a child suckling, the action, if not the pose, of Christ in the *Madonna Litta* (St Petersburg, Hermitage), executed in the early 1490s by an associate of Leonardo (probably Giovanni Antonio Boltraffio) to the master's designs. The pose of the leg to the right of **19** is close to that in the *Madonna Litta*, and both sheets may be first studies towards that painting.

The small study at lower left of **18** shows the infant raising his right hand in blessing, with his body twisted in the manner of the *Adoration of the Magi* (fig. 4), while at the centre he puts his fingers in his mouth, perhaps to eat a Eucharistic grape. Some of the studies to the right, of the limbs of a chubby child, are close in their details to the Child in Leonardo's *Benois Madonna* (also Hermitage), though that painting was probably executed several years earlier. The study at the centre of **19**, of an infant standing erect in strict profile, is related to Leonardo's proportion studies of around 1490 (**31–33**), when he started surveying the body systematically.

20

The drapery of a kneeling figure, c.1491–4

Brush and black ink, white heightening,
on pale blue prepared paper. 21.3 × 15.9 cm.
Melzi's 223. RCIN 912521

This appears to be a study for the angel's drapery in the second version of Leonardo's *Virgin of the Rocks*, the most protracted project of Leonardo's career. The commission to paint an altarpiece for the church of San Francesco Grande in Milan was signed by Leonardo and Ambrogio and Evangelista de' Predis in April 1483 – the earliest document of Leonardo's presence in the city. A first version (Paris, Louvre) was apparently complete within a few years, though it was not delivered, for unknown reasons; instead, a second version (fig. 7) was begun, probably in the early 1490s, and finally installed in San Francesco in 1508 after much legal wrangling.

The compositions of the two versions are generally the same, but there are many differences of detail. The drapery of the angel in the Paris version isolates his arm and head, and the expanse of red cloth exaggerates his posterior to an unfortunate degree. In this drawing Leonardo redesigned the angel for the second version, the pose more upright, and a swag of drapery from the right shoulder over the left hip and thigh to break the expanse of cloth. While substantial areas of the London painting were executed by an assistant, Leonardo's hand is perhaps most easily seen in this passage, an extraordinary depiction of light passing through and reflecting off a range of textiles.

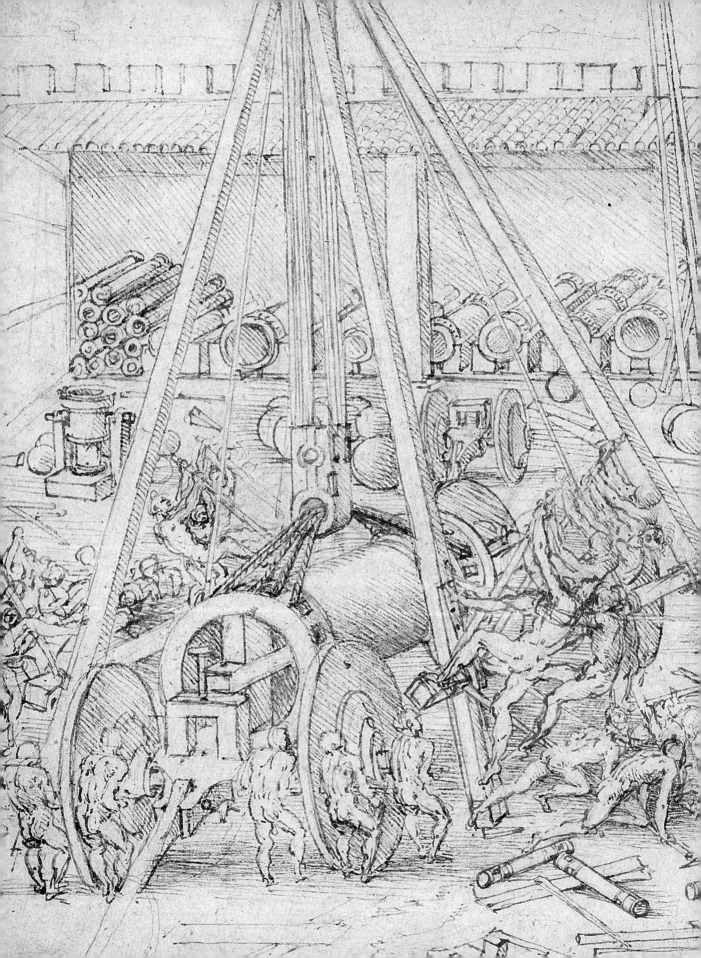

Engineering and weapons of the 1480s

21

Designs for chariots and weapons, c.1485

Stylus, pen and ink, wash.
20.0 × 27.8 cm. Melzi's 22. RCIN 912653

Leonardo's career coincided with the introduction of gunpowder into European warfare, and his many military drawings of the 1480s (**21–26**) include designs for both the old type of weapon – lances, chariots, enormous catapults and crossbows – and the new – guns, cannon and mortars. It is unlikely that any of these designs was put into practice, and indeed Leonardo could be dismissive of such inventions, noting that 'they often do no less damage to one's friends than to one's enemies'.[7] A number of his ideas were derived from woodcuts in a printed edition of Roberto Valturio's *De re militari*, a treatise on warfare written around 1450 and published from 1472 onwards, an edition of which was owned by Leonardo.

Detail of **26**

22 [OPPOSITE]

*Designs for gun-barrels
and mortars, c.1485*

Pen and ink. 28.2 × 20.5 cm.
RCIN 912652

23

Designs for weapons, c.1485

Pen and pale ink. 20.5 × 15.3 cm.
An early number 5 (not Melzi's).
RCIN 912651

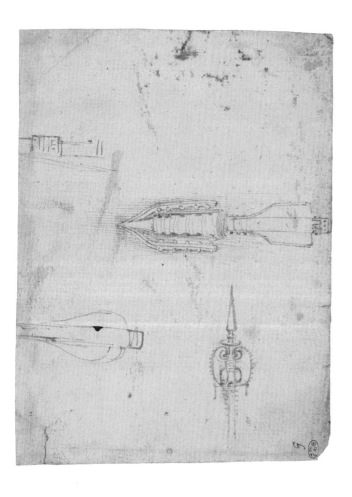

Writing a century later, Gian Paolo Lomazzo stated that Leonardo illustrated a book of military designs for the Milanese nobleman (and armourer to Ludovico Sforza) Gentile de' Borri. Alternatively Leonardo may have been considering producing a treatise of his own, with designs improving upon those illustrated in Valturio. **21** shows four such designs: a combined bow and shield, to protect the archer while allowing him to sight and shoot through holes in the shield; an apparatus to mount lances on the shoulders of a horse; and chariots with the wheels geared to a central vertical axle, so that when pulled into the ranks of the enemy the chariot would fling out weights or spiked clubs.

The largest drawing of **22** shows a box-shaped mortar mounted on a small boat, which would probably have capsized when the mortar was fired. The words 'gunpowder' and 'lime' are written on the boxes, and 'fire' in the spray from the circular barrel at centre. The mortars were therefore intended to discharge an incendiary substance known as 'Greek fire' to burn the rigging and sails of an enemy ship, a portion of which is visible at lower left. The long gun-barrels were conceived as fine pieces of engineering, cast in sections to be screwed together. At centre is a rotating cradle for mounting a gun with opposed barrels, so that one could be loaded while the other was fired (an idea found in Valturio). Below this is a lever-mounted tinder, operated by string from the end of a long pole – early gun-barrels frequently exploded in the face of the operator.

At the centre of **23** Leonardo drew an exploding projectile, with fins for accuracy, to be fired from a ballista (akin to a huge crossbow). On impact the rear of the missile would be driven into the front part, here shown in cutaway, to detonate its load of powder. At lower right is the head of a halberd with a spike flanked by two toothed blades, one of many such pole weapons drawn by Leonardo during the mid-1480s, with more concern for their decorative qualities than their effectiveness.

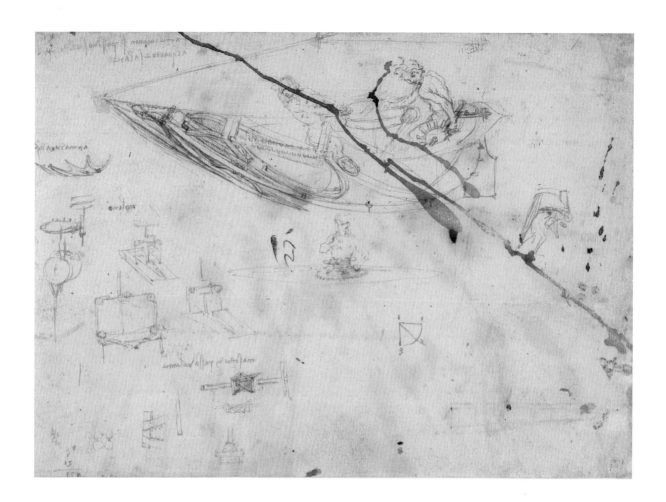

24
Designs for boats and other machinery, c.1485

Leadpoint, pen and ink. 20.8 × 28.8 cm.
Melzi's 27. RCIN 912649

25 [OPPOSITE]
Designs for boats, c.1485

Pen and ink. 14.2 × 21.4 cm.
Melzi's 18. RCIN 912650

The principal study in **24** depicts, in cutaway, a
mechanical boat operated by two men (one obscured
by ink dribbled across the sheet). The men seem to be
turning a large horizontal wheel, geared to a smaller
vertical wheel on a transverse axle, while the man in the
stern is leaning against another transverse axle bearing
a toothed wheel. How these axles are connected, if at
all, is not apparent, but there are many related drawings
in Leonardo's manuscripts, some of which have paddle
wheels either side of the boat (see **25** below). A chain
running from the middle of the boat to the bow may
be some folding mechanism, which would explain the
sketch to the right, of a man carrying on his back what
seems to be a folded boat. At centre is a figure with a
tight-fitting seal around his waist; long faint lines to
either side suggest this might be some sort of canoe.

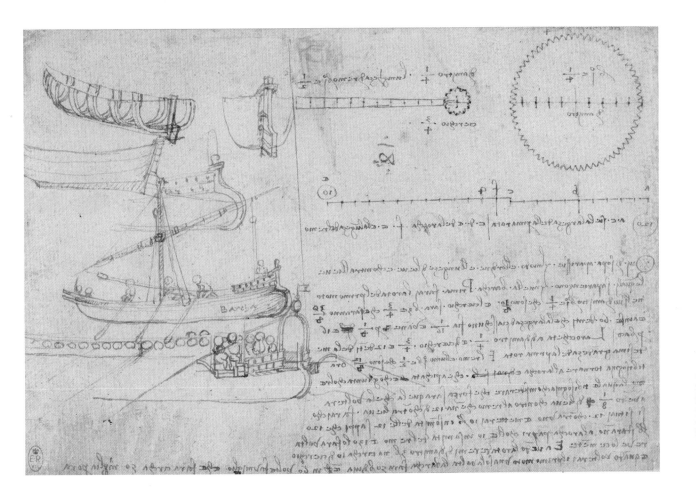

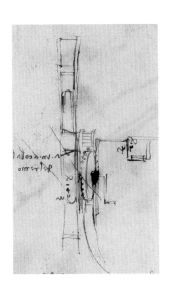

A geared paddle wheel.
Reverse of 24 (detail)

A paddle-boat.
Reverse of 25 (detail)

The drawing shown in **25** studies the construction of boats of various sizes – the line of circles in the lowest study are the heads of a bank of rowers. The notes describe the mechanism of a boat propelled by paddle wheels, as drawn on the reverse of this sheet and of **24** – a crank handle to turn a large toothed wheel, which is engaged with a smaller toothed wheel on the axle of a large paddle wheel, such that when the crank is turned the paddle wheel would spin quickly. Leonardo's calculations promise a speed of 50 miles per hour, but he seems not to understand that while such gears would increase the speed of rotation of the paddle wheel, they would also require proportionally greater turning force (torque) in the crank to do so.

26

A scene in an arsenal, c.1485–90

Pen and ink. 25.0 × 18.3 cm.
Melzi's 58. RCIN 912647
(Detail shown p. 48)

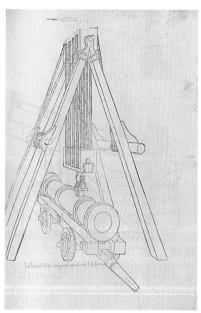

The drawing in **26** is the most formal of Leonardo's military drawings from the period, its composition derived from a woodcut in Valturio showing a framework and pulley for hoisting a cannon on and off its bogey (fig. 8). Here teams of nude men struggle with levers to take the weight of an enormous bombard, closely resembling the siege bombards that were a speciality of Ottoman foundries, such as the 'Dardanelles Gun' now at Fort Nelson, Portsmouth (and Leonardo has hardly exaggerated the size). Beyond are more gun barrels lying beneath a pitched roof against the wall of a fortress, with huge stone cannonballs, a mortar, ladders and lances.

Early scientific drawings

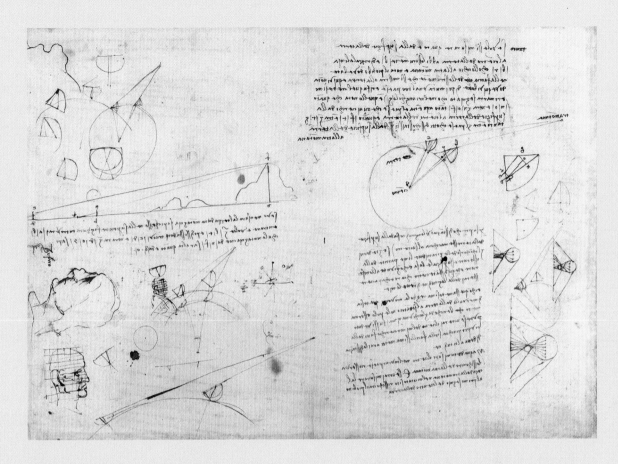

27

Geometrical and other studies, c.1482–5

Pen and ink. 29.4 × 41.5 cm. RCIN 919147

The sheet is typical of Leonardo's earliest scientific studies, an untidy combination of sketches, formal diagrams and irregular blocks of notes. At centre left he shows how the height of a mountain may be determined by measuring the angle of elevation of its summit from different points in the plain below. Other diagrams demonstrate the similar method of calculating the radius of the earth by measuring the elevation of the sun from different points on the earth's curved surface. The diagrams show that Leonardo considered the sun to be relatively close to the earth, and the calculations would require one to know that distance;

but the sun is in truth so distant that its rays may be considered parallel, simplifying the geometry – as surmised by the Greek mathematician Eratosthenes, who in the third century BC calculated the size of the earth using this method, by measuring midday shadows at different latitudes.

The three diagrams at lower right study the shadows cast by spheres of different sizes, a subject of enduring interest to Leonardo (**113**). Two male heads at lower left with grids superimposed are a first glimpse of Leonardo's proportional studies (**31–33**); the crude head alongside is not by Leonardo.

28

A ravine, c.1482–5

Pen and ink. 22.0 × 15.8 cm.
Melzi's 136. RCIN 912395

Scrubby trees cling to stratified rocks along the edge of the narrow ravine, the shallow water plays over rocks in the river bed, and at centre right the current has eroded the rock into smooth arcs. The landscape was probably drawn from the imagination, and the cartoonish waterfowl give an air of unreality. But what may appear fanciful actually depicts with geological accuracy the weathered pillars of sandstone and hard clay (*balze*) peculiar to the upper Arno valley, south-east of Florence. The drawing is probably contemporary with Leonardo's first *Virgin of the Rocks* (Paris, Louvre; see **20**), commissioned in Milan in 1483; and while it is not directly preparatory for that painting, the grotto in which Leonardo placed the holy group is modelled on such rock formations, remembered from his native Tuscany.

29

A sheet of miscellaneous studies, c.1490

Stylus, compasses, pen and ink, a little red chalk.
32.0 × 44.6 cm. RCIN 912283. (Detail shown pp. 2–3)

This large sheet has been seen as typifying Leonardo's effortless movement from subject to subject in his drawings, but few sheets cover such a range of material. First to be drawn were the two large geometrical diagrams, in which Leonardo played around with circles, arcs and triangles – the transformation and equivalence of areas bounded by such lines was an abiding hobby. Around these diagrams he fitted small studies of many of the subjects that were bubbling away in his mind in the years around 1490: a rearing horse with rider echoing the Sforza monument (**40–41**), and

a standing warrior; two sketches of a screw press; an old man in profile, his cloak merging with a study of trees; and a smaller geometrical diagram that morphs into mountain peaks. Below centre is a meticulously drawn blade of grass, and at top left an arum lily and two sketches of foliage. At centre right is a bank of strongly lit cumulus cloud, as studied in drawings and notes to the end of Leonardo's career (**199**). Below is a sketch of water falling into a pool, though the scale is hard to gauge – it could be a puddle, or a vast cloudburst comparable to the late *Deluges* (**188–197**).

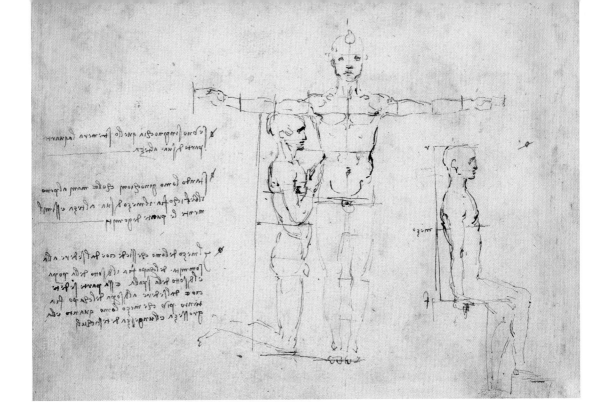

30 [OPPOSITE]

The fall of light on a face, c.1488

Pen and ink. 20.3 × 14.3 cm. RCIN 912604

During the 1480s Leonardo's interests diversified, and he started to assemble material towards a treatise on painting. His own paintings are notable for their elaborate treatment of shadows or *chiaroscuro*, and in **30** he sets out the geometrical principles of light and shade. The notes explain that where the light falls perpendicularly on the object, it will be most strongly illuminated; where it falls most obliquely, the object will be least strongly lit; and where no light is received it will be completely dark. The diagram at left shows the 'perspective' of shadows, radiating from the centre of an illuminating square window. The note above recommends that 'when you compose a picture take two points, one the point of sight, the other the source of light, and make them as distant as possible' – that is, a scene should be lit from the side, so that the objects are depicted in maximum relief.

31

The proportions of a standing, kneeling and sitting man, c.1490

Pen and ink. 15.9 × 20.8 cm. RCIN 919132

The system of human proportions in the central drawing of **31** follows that set out in the treatise *On Architecture* by the Roman architect Vitruvius (first century BC). Accordingly, the height of the man is equal to the span of his outstretched arms; a quarter of his height is the cubit, marked off horizontally at the knees, pubis and between the armpits, and vertically at the elbows and down the centre of the chest. The same proportions are seen in Leonardo's most famous drawing, the 'Vitruvian man' standing with arms outstretched in a square and circle (Venice, Accademia). The notes explain the two subsidiary diagrams: 'if a man kneels he will diminish by a quarter part of his height', and 'the umbilicus is [then] the middle of his height'; and 'the middle of a man who sits [...] is below the breast and below the shoulder'.

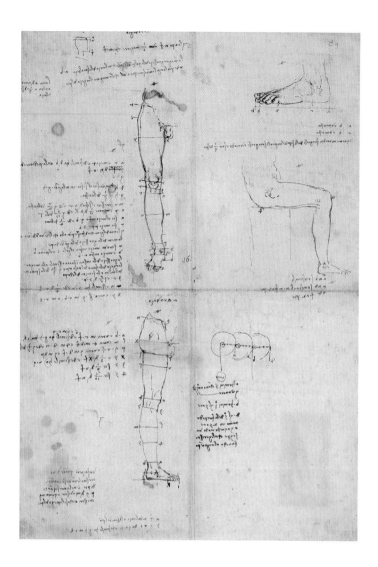

32

The proportions of the leg and foot, c.1490

Pen and ink. 40.0 × 28.0 cm.
RCIN 919136v

33 [OPPOSITE]

The proportions of the head, and a standing nude, c.1490

Metalpoint, pen and ink, on blue-grey prepared paper. 21.3 × 15.3 cm.
RCIN 912601

The simple precepts illustrated in **31** were discarded when, in **32**, Leonardo began to measure an individual, named as 'Caravaggio' and so from that town near Milan. The drawing is an early example of overwhelming detail in Leonardo's scientific investigations, with such explanatory notes as '*mn* increases by ⅙ from *ac* and is ⁷⁄₁₂ of a head'; '*op* is ¹⁄₁₀ less than *dk* and is ⁶⁄₁₇ of a head'; 'the hollow on the outside of the knee at *r* is higher than the hollow on the inside at *a* by half the thickness of the leg at the foot'; and so on.

In **33** Leonardo attempts instead to find correspondences of length between parts of the face, without resorting to fractions: 'It is as far from *a* to *b*, from the start of the hair at the front to the line of the top of the head, as it is from *c* to *d*, from the lower end of the nose to the junction of the lips at the front of the mouth,' and so on. He inked over the metalpoint outlines to clarify the diagram, adjusting the back of the cranium to make the depth of the head (excluding the nose) equal to the height of the face (from chin to hairline). The eye is at the mid-point of the head, and the face is divided into three equal sections, from the base of the chin to the base of the nose, thence to the brow, and thence to the hairline.

The practical difficulties that an artist would have encountered in making use of such measurements cannot have been lost on Leonardo, and after 1490 he largely abandoned detailed proportional studies.

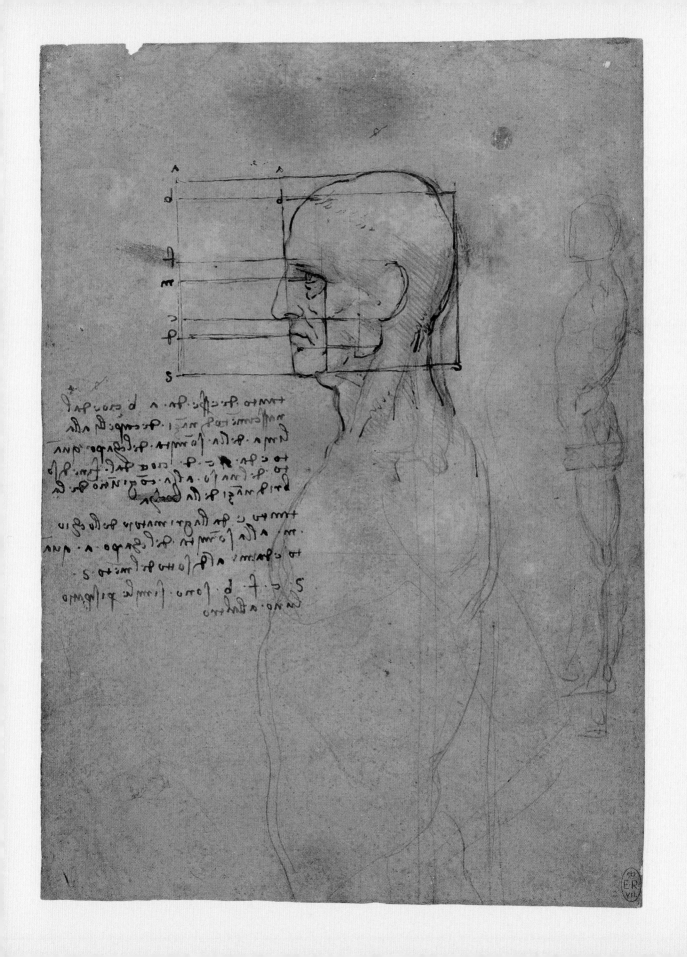

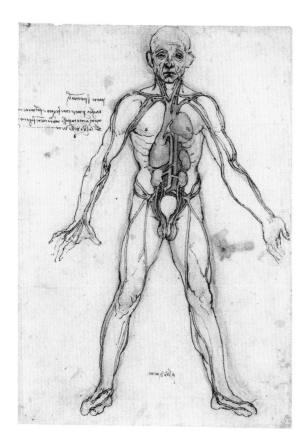

34
The major organs and vessels,
c.1485–90

Black chalk or charcoal, pen and ink, brown
and green wash. 27.8 × 19.7 cm. RCIN 912597

35 [OPPOSITE]
The hemisection of a man
and woman in the act of coition,
c.1490–92

Pen and ink. 27.6 × 20.4 cm. RCIN 919097v

In the late 1480s Leonardo proposed a treatise on
human anatomy. The human body was of course the
principal subject matter of the Renaissance artist, and
Leonardo quickly realised that it was far too complex
for a mere chapter of his treatise on painting (**30–33**).
In time anatomy would become Leonardo's greatest
scientific pursuit, and though he never completed his
treatise, his later studies (**119–143**) mark him out as one
of the great scientists of the Renaissance.

The illustration in **34** was drawn before Leonardo
had carried out any significant human dissection,
and summarises traditional beliefs about the major
organs and vessels. The arterial and venous systems
were believed to be essentially separate: the heart was
thought to produce 'vital spirit', the life force, which
was distributed throughout the body by the arterial
system, while the liver was the source of nutrition or
'natural spirit', creating blood that was distributed by
the veins to nourish the body. A quarter of a century
later, Leonardo was to place the heart at the centre
of both the arterial and venous systems, but he never
moved beyond this essential separation of the systems
and their functions (see **140–143**).

Leonardo's forerunners differed on whether conception
involved a material union, a spiritual union, or both.
Plato, for example, believed that the 'seed' was a spiritual
entity in the brain and spinal cord, and here Leonardo
notes that 'Avicenna [the eleventh-century Persian
philosopher Ibn Sīnā] claims that the soul begets the
soul, and the body the body'. But here Leonardo seems
to depict an arrangement whereby *three* components are
involved in conception, following the medieval division
of the body: in the man he has drawn channels into the
penis from the brain via the spinal cord (to transmit an
'animal' element, or soul), from the heart (a 'spiritual'
element), and from the testes (a 'material' element).

In the woman, the spine bifurcates and a branch
of the spinal cord passes directly into the uterus, to
transmit the woman's soul to the child, but the ovaries
and heart are not drawn, and it is thus questionable
whether, at this stage of his career, Leonardo believed
that there was an equal contribution to conception
from the female.

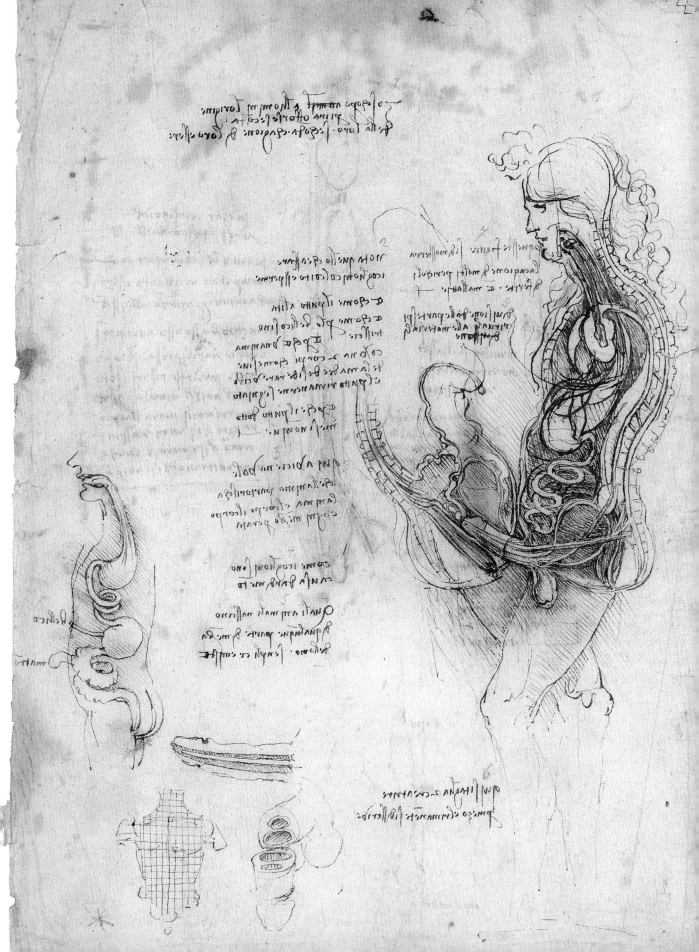

36
The anatomy of a bear's foot, c.1488–90

Metalpoint, pen and ink, white heightening, on
blue-grey prepared paper. 16.1 × 13.7 cm. RCIN 912372
(Detail shown p. 17)

During the latter part of the 1480s, Leonardo dissected
the left hind leg of a bear, an animal then widespread
in the mountains of Italy. His interest in the bear may
have been due to its plantigrade gait – walking with its
feet flat on the ground, like a human. This dissection
therefore gave Leonardo an insight into the anatomy
of the foot at a time when he had little access to human
material, and, 20 years later, when he was able to dissect
the human hand and foot (**131**, **136**), he recalled the
details of the bear's anatomy.

 The drawing shows with some accuracy the bones,
muscles and tendons of the bear's lower leg and foot,
with the big toe, claw raised, away from the viewer.
Unlike many of his other anatomical studies at this
time, which rely on traditional beliefs, Leonardo had
no preconceptions about how a bear's foot should be
constructed, and so drew his subject with clear-sighted
objectivity.

37
The skull sectioned, 1489

Traces of black chalk, pen and ink.
18.8 × 13.4 cm. RCIN 919057

The drawings shown in **37** and **38** are taken from a
notebook of 44 folios, the Anatomical Manuscript B,
used by Leonardo for his anatomical studies during
two periods 20 years apart (for the later drawings see
119–122). He began the notebook in April 1489 with
drawings of a human skull, cut in a variety of sections to
study the relationship between its external and internal
structure. Leonardo wished to determine the paths of
the sensory nerves and the location within the brain
of the *senso comune*, the supposed site at which the
senses converged – and for one who believed in the
primacy of sensory information, the centre of human
experience, and the site of the soul.

 In the upper drawing of **37**, Leonardo places the *senso
comune* at the intersection of three orthogonal lines,
just behind where the optic nerves enter the brain.
The lower drawing shows the skull sawn in half, with
the cervical vertebrae included schematically. Leonardo
locates the *senso comune* at the mid-point of the height
of the skull and a third of the way back – resisting the
temptation to place it exactly halfway from front to
back, which would have been even more harmonious.

 In **38**, Leonardo shows the skull sawn first down the
middle, then across the front of the right side. With the
two halves juxtaposed, the viewer can locate the facial
cavities in relation to the surface features – the frontal
sinus within the brow, the orbit of the eye, the nasal
cavity, the maxillary sinus in the cheek, and the mouth.
Leonardo believed all except the frontal sinus to be a
third of the depth of the skull, each terminating below
the *senso comune*. In the left margin Leonardo drew,
described and enumerated the different types of teeth,
molar, premolar, canine and incisor.

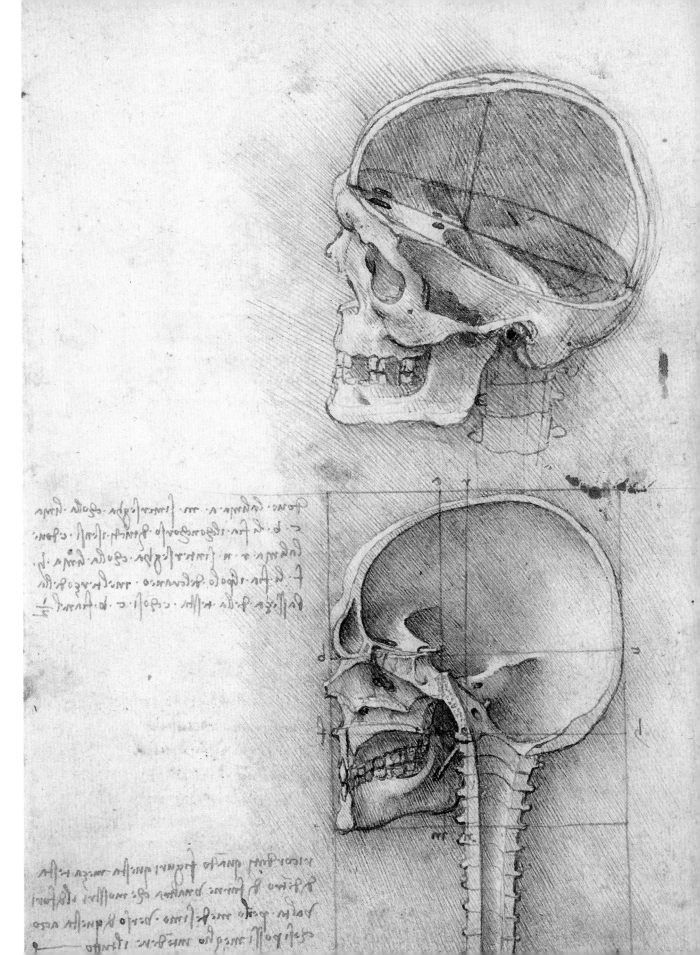

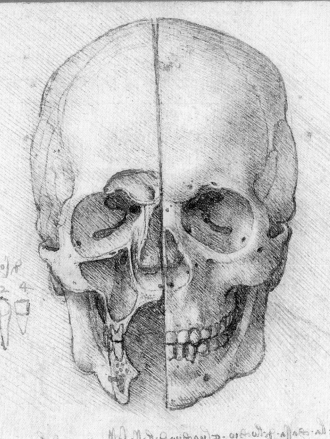

38 [OPPOSITE]

The skull sectioned, 1489

Traces of black chalk, pen and ink.
19.0 × 13.7 cm. RCIN 919058v

39

The layers of the scalp,
and the cerebral ventricles,
c.1490–92

Red chalk, pen and ink.
20.3 × 15.3 cm. RCIN 912603

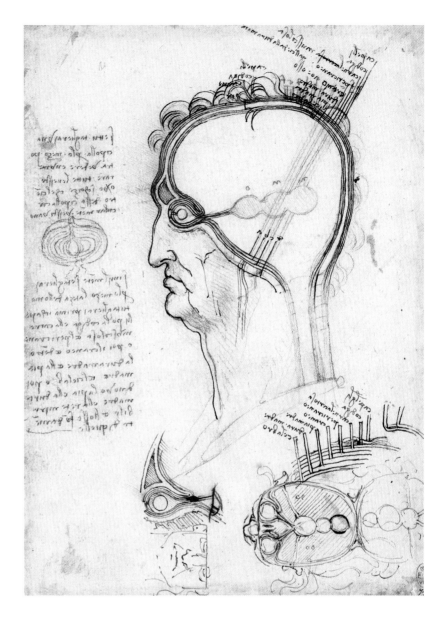

The principal drawing imagines the head sectioned through the middle, its layers likened to those of an onion, and listed as 'hair; scalp; muscular flesh; pericranium arising from the dura mater; cranium, that is, bone; dura mater; pia mater; brain'. Leonardo correctly shows the meningeal membrane of the dura mater extending along the optic nerve to the eye.

Within the brain, Leonardo drew the cerebral ventricles as three bulbous cavities. These were believed to house the mental faculties: the first was where the mind's 'raw material' was gathered – the *senso comune* (see **37–38**), imagination and fantasy; in the second this information was processed, through reasoning and so on; and the third was where the results were stored, in the memory. At lower right the head is seen from above with the crown of the head flipped back, the optic and auditory nerves converging on the first ventricle. But Leonardo was unconvinced by this arrangement, repeatedly trying different layouts, and he later abandoned the traditional system of the localisation of mental faculties (**124**).

The Sforza monument

FIG.9
Antonio del Pollaiuolo,
*A design for the Sforza monument, c.*1480–84.
Black chalk, pen and ink, wash,
pricked through. 28.8 × 25.5 cm.
New York, Metropolitan Museum of Art,
Robert Lehman Collection

During the 1480s Ludovico Sforza, ruler (though not yet Duke) of Milan, commissioned Leonardo to execute a bronze equestrian monument, well over life size, to his father Francesco (1401–66). An equestrian monument to Francesco – a military commander who had married into the ruling Visconti family and in time became Duke of Milan – had been conceived in 1473 by Galeazzo Maria Sforza, Ludovico's eldest brother, but nothing was done at that time. Galeazzo Maria was assassinated in 1476 and Ludovico was soon sent into exile, but on his return to Milan in 1479 and usurpation of power from his young nephew Gian Galeazzo, Ludovico revived the project of the equestrian monument.

Ludovico's first choice for the commission seems to have been the Florentine Antonio del Pollaiuolo, an experienced sculptor in metal, if not yet on a grand scale; the most experienced bronze sculptor in Italy, Leonardo's former associate Andrea del Verrocchio, was then fully occupied on the Colleoni monument (see **11**). Two drawings by Pollaiuolo for the project show Francesco in modern armour, with the horse rearing over a fallen figure (fig. 9). Those designs probably date no later than 1484, when Pollaiuolo began work on the tomb of Pope Sixtus IV in Rome, leaving Ludovico to seek another artist. Letters from Lorenzo de' Medici to Ludovico suggest that the latter had requested sculptors be sent from Florence (for unstated reasons) in April 1484.

40
A design for an equestrian monument, c.1485–8

Metalpoint on blue-grey prepared paper.
11.6 × 10.3 cm. RCIN 912357

FIG.10
After Leonardo, *Designs for the Sforza monument*, c.1490. Engraving. 21.7 × 16.0 cm.
London, British Museum

That Ludovico was in need of a sculptor was clearly public knowledge, for in a draft letter to Ludovico seeking employment, probably of the mid-1480s, Leonardo claimed 'I can carry out sculpture in marble, bronze or clay [...] as well as any other. [...] The bronze horse may be taken in hand, to the immortal glory and eternal honour of the prince your father of happy memory, and of the illustrious house of Sforza.'[8] Although he could not cite any sculpture that he had himself completed, Leonardo's years with Verrocchio may have been decisive in securing the commission.

Leonardo's early drawings for the monument differ little in iconography from those of Pollaiuolo. **40** is a likeness of Francesco in armour, wielding a baton on a rearing horse, lacking only the fallen foe. Though it is carefully finished, its small scale would be inadequate for presentation to a patron; it corresponds closely (other than the garb of the rider) with one of four designs in a contemporary engraving (fig. 10), all of which must record similar drawings by Leonardo, and it is possible that **40** was drawn specifically as a model for the engraver.

A fallen foe appears in **41**, a shield raised over his head, but the poses of horse and rider are essentially the same as in **40**. Leonardo has drawn the rider – now a featureless figure rather than a likeness of Francesco – with his arms in several alternative positions, the left holding the reins before his chest or down at his hip, the right thrusting a baton either forwards or backwards. Studies of water and geometry on the reverse of the sheet can be dated to the latter half of the 1480s: a decade after Ludovico had seized power in Milan, the monument to his father was still no more than a design on paper.

41
A design for an equestrian monument, c.1485–8

Metalpoint on blue prepared paper.
14.8 × 18.5 cm. Melzi's *114*. RCIN 912358

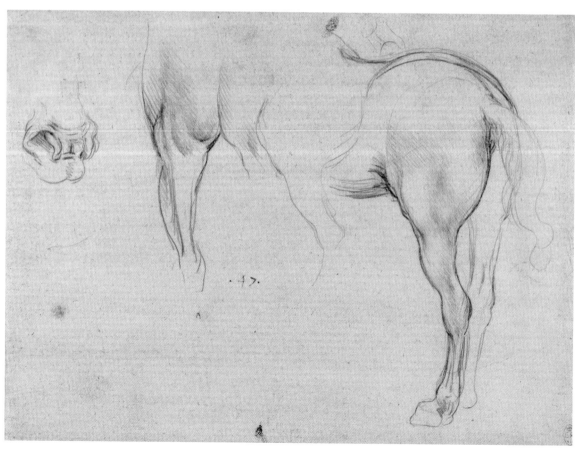

42 [OPPOSITE, ABOVE]

Studies of a horse, c.1490

Metalpoint on pale pinkish-buff prepared
paper. 20.0 × 28.4 cm. Melzi's *48*. RCIN 912317

43 [OPPOSITE, BELOW]

Studies of a horse, c.1490

Metalpoint on pale pinkish-buff prepared
paper. 18.0 × 24.3 cm. Melzi's *47*. RCIN 912310

44

Studies of a horse, c.1490

Metalpoint on blue-grey prepared paper.
21.4 × 16.0 cm. Melzi's *103*. RCIN 912321
(Detail shown p. 68)

In July 1489 the Florentine ambassador in Milan wrote
to Lorenzo de' Medici that Ludovico requested the
names of other artists who might be more suited to
execute the 'great bronze horse', as he was not confident
of Leonardo's abilities – ironically our first documentary
reference to Leonardo being in Ludovico's employ.[9]
Lorenzo replied that there was no-one in Florence
suitable, and in time Leonardo overcame Ludovico's
doubts, for in April 1490 he recorded, 'I recommended
the horse'.[10] An important step in reassuring Ludovico
may have been the switch from a rearing horse, unprecedented in a large-scale bronze, to a more conventional
walking horse, with left foreleg raised and right hind
leg advanced. This new pose is seen in a tiny sketch at
lower right of **42**, inspired by the Roman equestrian
monument known as the Regisole (since destroyed) in
Pavia, south of Milan.

Leonardo now started to study the form of the
horse intensively: drawings from the life in casual
poses (**42–43**), details of legs in the intended pose of
the monument, and surveys of the horse in orthogonal
views (**44–45**). The proportions of the horse evolve from
a delicate, skittish type to a heavier build with a more
classical head. Leonardo measured individual horses
minutely, using as his unit the horse's head divided into
sixteenths; inscriptions on the drawings record that **46**
depicts a large jennet (a Spanish breed) and **47** a Sicilian,
both belonging to Galeazzo Sanseverino, captain-general
of the Milanese army and son-in-law of Ludovico Sforza.
The Sicilian, still an admired cavalry horse, appears
in several of Leonardo's measured studies and was
probably the breed intended for the monument.

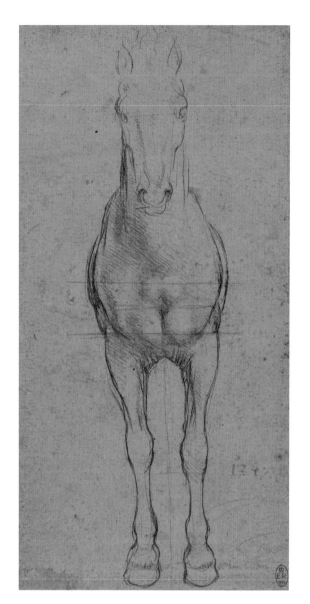

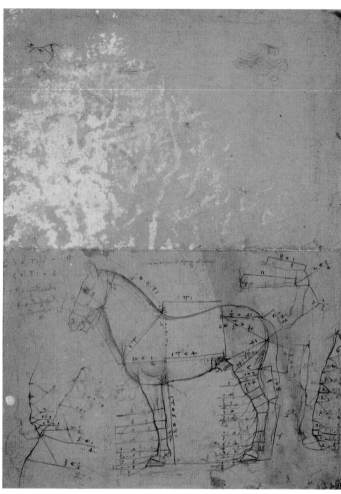

45
A study of a horse, c.1490

Metalpoint on blue-grey prepared paper.
22.1 × 11.0 cm. Melzi's *129*. RCIN 912290

46
A horse in left profile,
with measurements, c.1490

Metalpoint and pen and ink on blue-grey
prepared paper, the outlines incised; sharply folded,
the upper half damaged by damp. 32.4 × 23.7 cm.
RCIN 912319. (Detail shown pp. 34–5)

47 [OPPOSITE]
A horse's left foreleg,
with measurements, c.1490–92

Leadpoint, pen and ink, staining.
25.0 × 18.7 cm. Melzi's *41*. RCIN 912294

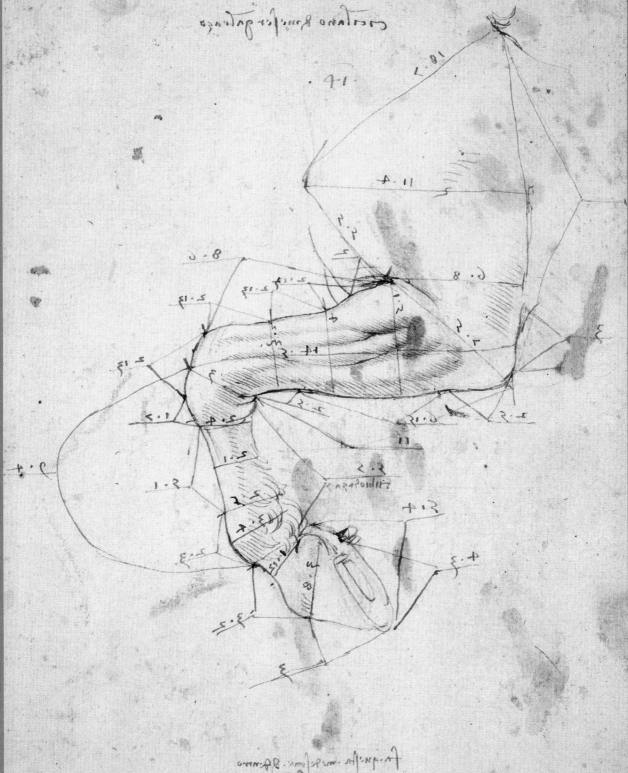

Over the next few years Leonardo built a full-size clay model of the horse, from which he took sectional moulds to construct a matrix for the casting. The figure of Francesco Sforza – surely the most important aspect from Ludovico's point of view – seems hardly to have entered Leonardo's thoughts: the monument is always referred to in his notes simply as 'the horse', and the modelling of the rider must have been deferred. Nonetheless the casting of the horse alone was a huge challenge, requiring the building of an entire foundry, and in October 1492 Leonardo may have sought advice on this from the Florentine architect and engineer Giuliano da Sangallo, then in Milan. The sheet of technical studies for the casting, **48**, has sketches at upper left and centre right giving a cross-section of the foundry, the mould buried underground and the horse shown as a cylinder with two straight legs pointing upwards. The largest drawings depict gears and pulley blocks to haul the mould out of the ground after casting (perhaps inspired by Valturio's cannon-hoist, fig. 8). The small drawings of branching lines are channels through which the molten metal would run, and the view of the separated halves of the structure at lower right shows tie-bars to secure the pieces of the mould.

Leonardo noted in December 1493 that he had decided to cast the horse on its side, rather than upside-down, and work was presumably continuing slowly on the practical arrangements for the casting. But the following year the French forces of Charles VIII invaded Italy, and Ludovico sent the bronze assembled for Leonardo's horse – perhaps 75 tons – to his brother-in-law Ercole d'Este in Ferrara, to make cannon. Leonardo may have continued to work on the casting apparatus in parallel with his painting of the *Last Supper* (fig. 11), but without bronze there could be no monument, which remained in abeyance for the rest of the decade. In a draft letter to Ludovico of the later 1490s, Leonardo wrote frustratedly, 'of the horse I will say nothing, for I know the times'.[11]

In September 1499, French forces took Milan and deposed Ludovico. Leonardo's clay model was used for target practice by the French troops and destroyed, and he left Milan that December, recording laconically in a notebook, 'the Duke lost his state, his property and his liberty, and none of his works was finished'. Two years later the Ferrarese ambassador in Milan requested the deteriorating moulds from the French authorities, with the aim of using them to cast an equestrian monument to Ercole d'Este, but nothing apparently came of this. The monument to Francesco Sforza, on which Leonardo had laboured for so many years, had come to nothing, and lines on the reverse of **48**, copied out by Leonardo from Dante's *Inferno,* take on a peculiarly prophetic quality: 'He who, without Fame, burns his life to waste / leaves no more vestige of himself on earth than / wind-blown smoke, or foam upon the water.'[12]

48

Studies of casting apparatus, and miscellaneous notes, c.1492–3

Pen and ink, red chalk. 27.8 × 19.1 cm.
Melzi's 24. RCIN 912349

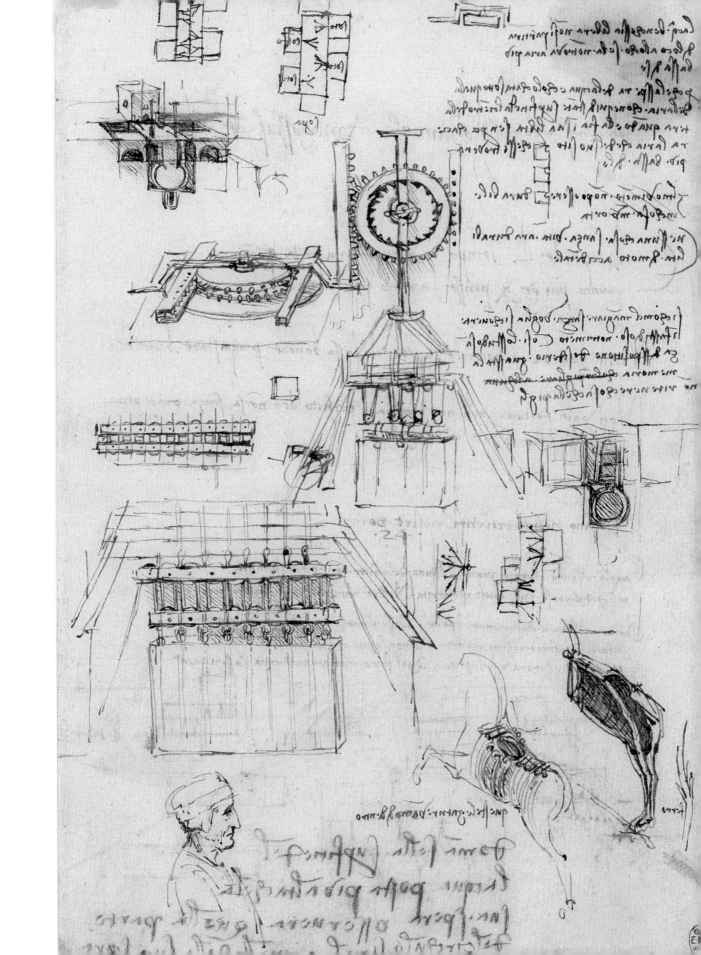

Entertainments

Throughout Leonardo's life, and particularly in the years around 1490, he sketched countless grotesque heads. They can be seen as a counterpart to his investigations of ideal human proportion (31–33), distorting those ideals of beauty to create images of 'ideal ugliness'. Leonardo had no intention of introducing such grotesques into his writings or his paintings – they were essentially amusements, for himself and his associates, and probably for the Sforza court too.

In **49**, a fierce old man with spare and deeply lined features faces a vain old woman, hair pulled back and bodice laced so tightly that her breasts bulge out.

A contrast of types was intended: he has thin lips sucked in over missing teeth, whereas she has fleshy lips; his bony chin answers her receding double chin; his beetling brow opposes her sloping forehead. Their difference in scale indicates that Leonardo did not initially conceive of the figures as interacting, but as an afterthought he sketched in the right arm of the woman, her hand to the man's chin in a romantic gesture. Leonardo thereby turned them into a pair of ridiculous aged lovers, a parody of the opposed profiles of married couples that were common in fifteenth-century portraiture.

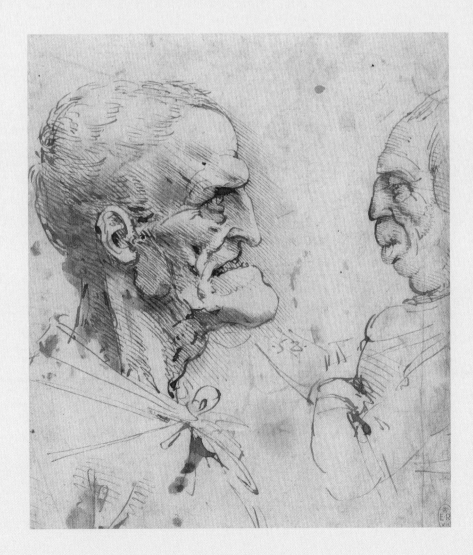

49 [RIGHT]

Two grotesque profiles,
c.1485–90

Pen and ink, wash. 16.3 × 14.3 cm.
Melzi's 52. RCIN 912490

50

A satire on aged lovers, c.1490

Leadpoint, pen and pale ink. 26.2 × 12.3 cm.
RCIN 912449

51

A caricature of a bald fat man, c.1485–90

Pen and ink. 16.0 × 13.5 cm. Melzi's 24.
RCIN 912489

The theme of aged lovers recurs in **50**: the woman in
a low-cut bodice now has an ostentatious headdress,
while the gap-toothed man, gazing ardently at her,
wears a similarly old-fashioned outsized hat. He appears
to be offering the woman a flower, and the drawing
is therefore a rather cruel satire on the vanity and
ridiculousness of the elderly behaving like young lovers.

The corpulent man in **51** is not one of Leonardo's
stock types, and the evident speed with which he was
drawn suggests that this may be a sketch of a specific
individual, the nose and lower lip exaggerated for comic
effect, and thus one of Leonardo's few true caricatures.

52 [LEFT]

A man tricked by Gypsies, c.1493

Pen and ink. 26.0 × 20.5 cm. RCIN 912495
(Detail shown p. 78)

53 [BELOW]

Two heads of grotesque animals,
c.1490–95

Black chalk, pen and ink. 13.8 × 17.4 cm.
Melzi's 40. RCIN 912367

The man at the centre of **52** raises his right arm to have his palm read by the old woman in traditional Gypsy dress on the right – unfortunately the sheet was cut at an early date and the palm-reading trimmed off. While the man is distracted, the grinning Gypsy on the left reaches under his sleeve to steal his purse. The two figures behind stare with hooded brow or laugh hysterically, adding to the sense of claustrophobic menace.

Gypsies had arrived in western Europe around 1420, claiming to be penitent pilgrims from Egypt but soon acquiring a reputation for fortune-telling and theft. Leonardo's drawing dates from a period of particular hostility to Gypsies in Milan, and they were banished from the Duchy of Lombardy in April 1493, the first such edict in Italy. The drawing was therefore a satire on current affairs, probably made for the entertainment of the Sforza court. It seems to have left Leonardo's hands and became one of his best-known compositions, serving as the basis for paintings by Giorgione and (possibly) Albrecht Dürer in Venice and Quentin Massys in Antwerp. By the 1580s it was in circulation in Milan and was presumably acquired then by Pompeo Leoni, separately from Melzi's inheritance. The young Caravaggio was serving his apprenticeship in the city at that time and may have known the drawing, and indeed this was to become a common subject in Caravaggesque painting across Europe in the seventeenth century.

On the right is a long-haired hound with a grotesquely long lower lip, a sign of inanity. The other head is a composite (like the dragons in **5**), with a mouth like a pug dog, a lion's mane, ears like a shaggy bear, and strange wrinkled flaps from the brow hanging down the cheeks. The bit in its mouth and bridle may suggest that this was a study for a fantastic mask to be worn by a costumed servant pulling a chariot or float in some festivity (cf. **176**), perhaps in January 1491 to celebrate the wedding of Ludovico Sforza and Beatrice d'Este, for which we know Leonardo designed costumes of wild men.

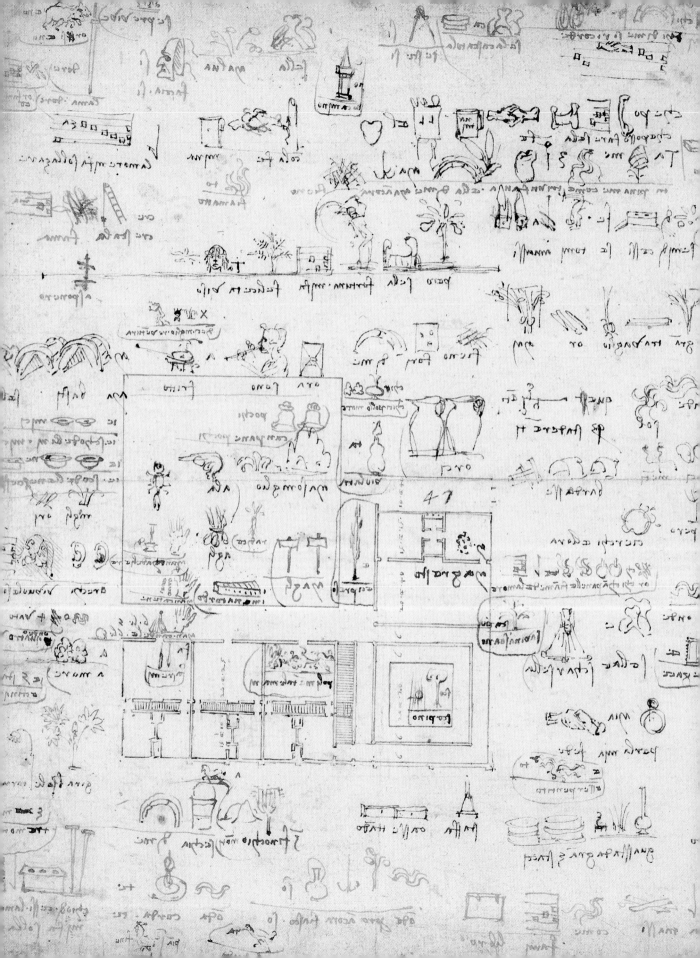

54
Pictographs, and an architectural plan, c.1490

Stylus, pen and ink. 30.0 × 25.3 cm.
Melzi's 47. RCIN 912692v

Pictorial puns, rebuses and other cryptograms were beloved of the Renaissance. Here Leonardo tried his hand at pictographs, playful 'picture writing' formed from a combination of objects which stand for themselves, objects and symbols that sound the same as other words, and a few linking letters, with the solution written below each line.

Many of the sequences are fragmentary phrases on the trials of love, the standard theme of courtly poetry. For instance, at upper right are the letters *che po*; a bone (*osso*); the musical notes *fa re*; a saddle (*sella*); a handshake, representing good faith (*fede*, or *fe'*); a measuring cup (*mina*); an ecclesiastical mitre (*mitra*); the letters *el*; and a heart (*cuore*). This gives *Che posso fare se la femina mi trae'l cuore*, 'What can I do if the woman plucks my heart?' Below this are the letters *Ta*; a pine cone (*pigna*); the letters *me*; some strands of hair (*come*); the numbers 3 and 1 (*tre uno*); a bean (*fava*); a branch of the plant *ella*; two sections of an arch (*dime*, in Milanese dialect); the letters *Ma*; an anchor (*ancora*); and some scribble to represent hay (*fieno*): thus *Tapina me, come triunfava ella di me! Ma ancora fieno*, 'Wretched me, how she triumphed over me! But still I will be'. And so on.

Leonardo drew the pictograms over an architectural plan, probably a project to remodel the Corte Vecchia in Milan, to the south of the Duomo, where he had his lodgings and workshop.

55
An architectural allegory, and designs for a stage set, c.1495

Pen and ink. 15.7 × 21.5 cm. RCIN 912497

A monstrous head, legs and tail have burst out of a large classical building, which pursues a man towards a flying woman surrounded by angels. She holds her arm over him in a gesture of protection; in her hand is what may be a pair of dividers, in which case she would be the personification of Architecture, perhaps then protecting the man (an architect? Leonardo himself?) from the terrors of an out-of-control building project.

Turning the sheet anticlockwise, we see a representation of the heavens, with a figure seated on a globe surrounded by flames, and small objects or rays of light falling through the clouds below. The pen style seems to be that of the 1490s (cf. **56**), and the drawing may be related to Leonardo's production of Baldassare Taccone's comedy *Danaë*, staged in the Milanese residence of Gianfrancesco Sanseverino in January 1496. Leonardo's cast list with a sketch of a stage set survives (New York, Metropolitan Museum), and the present drawing might depict Jupiter in the heavens, sending down the shower of gold in which guise he seduced the princess Danaë.

The Last Supper

Leonardo's greatest painting to reach completion was the *Last Supper* (fig. 11) in the refectory of Santa Maria delle Grazie in Milan, a revolutionary exercise in the depiction of emotion that combines the Institution of the Eucharist with the reaction of the Disciples to Christ's announcement of his imminent betrayal. The monastery church was a focus of Sforza patronage, and heraldic arms painted above the *Last Supper* testify that it was commissioned by Ludovico, who was reported to dine in the refectory twice a week.

In 1492 work began on a new tribune for the church, designed by Donato Bramante, to house the tombs of Ludovico and his wife Beatrice d'Este, and Leonardo's sketch **56** is of around the same date. He probably spent much time on the painting only after work on the Sforza horse had been suspended in late 1494; by June 1497 Ludovico was pressing Leonardo to finish the mural, and the dedication to Ludovico of Luca Pacioli's treatise *De divina proportione*, dated February 1498, implies that the painting was then complete. Leonardo executed the *Last Supper* in an experimental technique combining oil, tempera and varnish (he seems never to have worked in fresco), and it was soon deteriorating. Subsequent restorations culminated in a recent radical cleaning to remove later overpaint, and what we see now is a ghost of Leonardo's intentions.

FIG.11
The Last Supper, c.1494–8.
Tempera and oil on plaster.
460 × 880 cm.
Milan, Santa Maria delle Grazie

Detail of **57**

The drawing in **56** is the only true compositional study known for the mural. Leonardo's challenge was to integrate 13 men in a harmonious composition while differentiating them in their poses and facial types: a passage in Leonardo's notebook of c.1493–4 lists possible attitudes and actions, and an uncharacteristically stiff drawing in Venice that must be related to the project seems to be a similar assemblage of individual responses. At upper left of **56** are perhaps ten figures seated at the table, with Judas on the near side. To the right is a study for the central group, with Judas rising from his seat to take the bread from Christ, St John asleep on the table, and another Disciple in a gesture of astonishment. St John is sketched again immediately below, with a quick notation of two Disciples, one speaking in the other's ear. The studies of arcading and octagons might conceivably be related to the building projects at Santa Maria delle Grazie.

56 [OPPOSITE]

Sketches for the Last Supper, and other studies, c.1492–4

Pen and ink. 26.0 × 21.0 cm.
Melzi's 59. RCIN 912542

We have no trace of the process by which Leonardo moved beyond this rough sketch, and the few other surviving drawings were made once Leonardo had arrived at his extraordinary final composition. Only one head study is from the life, **57**, for the figure of St James, second to the right of Christ. The red chalk is coarsely and rapidly handled, to capture the spontaneity of his model's pose and expression. In the painting the figure is bearded and holds his arms wide in horror, but the face is ruined and, as here, it is uncertain whether St James casts his eyes down or stares straight at Christ. The architectural sketches on the sheet are probably studies for modifications to the Castello Sforzesco in Milan.

The other head studies come from a later stage of the creative process in which Leonardo fixed the image, perhaps unconsciously expunging the quirks of reality such that the features approximate closely to his standard types (**4**, **163**). The spontaneity of **57** is replaced in **58** by uniform finish and a heavily drawn outline, and the features have been idealised, taking the figure out of the real world and into the divine.

57

The head of St James, and architectural sketches, c.1495

Red chalk, pen and ink. 25.2 × 17.2 cm.
Melzi's 44. RCIN 912552. (Detail shown p. 84)

58

The head of St Philip, c.1495

Black chalk. 19.0 × 15.0 cm. Melzi's 27.
RCIN 912551

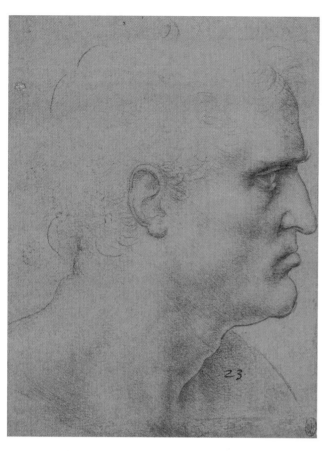

59
The head of St Bartholomew,
c.1495 or later

Red chalk on red prepared paper.
19.3 × 14.8 cm. Melzi's 23. RCIN 912548

60
The head of Judas,
c.1495 or later

Red chalk on red prepared paper.
18.0 × 15.0 cm. Melzi's 33. RCIN 912547

The remaining head studies represent a further step still in the creative process – **59** probably for St Bartholomew at far left; **60** for Judas, recoiling with guilt, three to the left of Christ; and two accurate copies of Leonardo's lost study for St Simon (RCINS 912549, 912550). These may be definitive drawings for Leonardo to consult while working (there is no evidence that he used a full-scale cartoon for the painting), or even 'fair copies' by Leonardo, intended to preserve his invention for future reference. Their careful finish has led to doubts about their authenticity, and while they are drawn with Leonardo's usual sensitivity, the profile of Judas may have been strengthened by a later hand. The only drapery study for the *Last Supper* is **61**, for the arm of St Peter twisted behind his back as he leans over Judas's shoulder. The chalk is handled with a softness and sense of inner life, of cloth moving over living flesh, quite different from **20** of just a few years before, and looking forward 20 years to the *St Anne* studies (**157–159**).

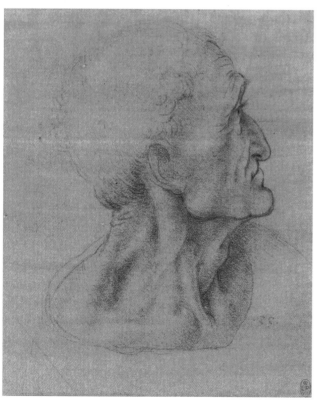

61
The arm of St Peter, c.1495

Black chalk, white heightening.
16.6 × 15.5 cm. Melzi's 224. RCIN 912546

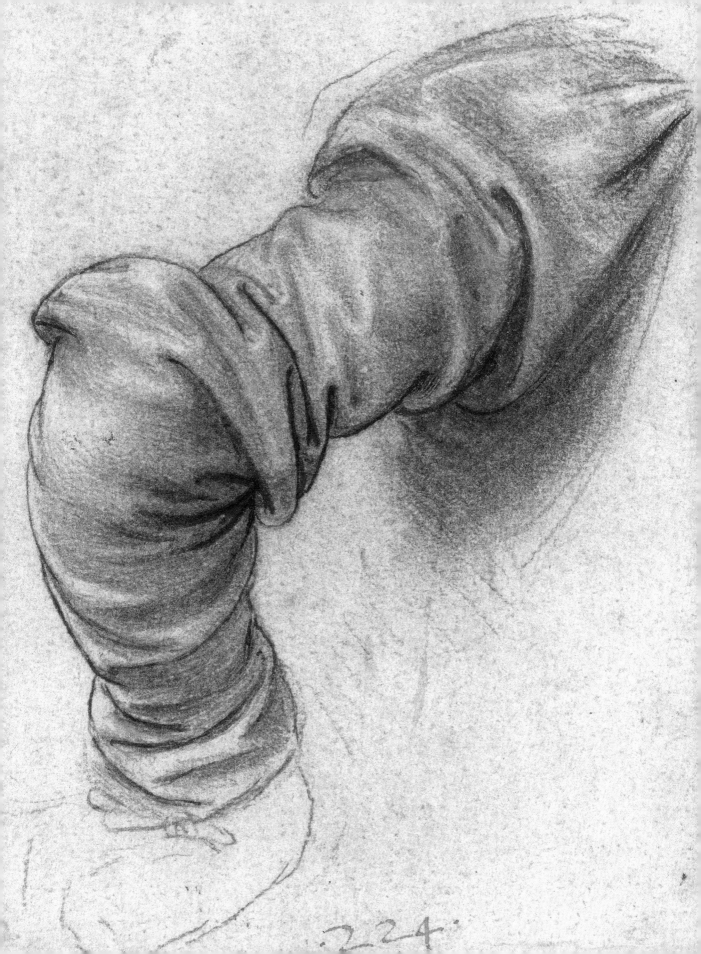

224

Works in Florence, 1500–1506

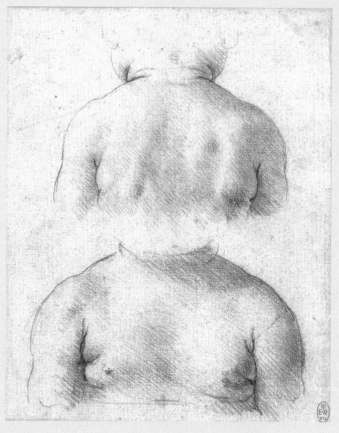

62

The bust of a child in profile,
c.1500

Red chalk. 10.0 × 10.0 cm.
Melzi's 3. RCIN 912519

63

The bust of a child from front
and back, c.1500

Red chalk. 16.5 × 13.6 cm. RCIN 912567

These two drawings must be related, for the chest of the
child terminates at the same horizontal line in all three
studies. The obvious context would be a terracotta bust
of the Christ Child or Infant Baptist, common during the
Renaissance as suitable exemplars in children's nurseries.
While no such bust by Leonardo is known – indeed, no
surviving sculpture is generally accepted as being by
the artist – the Milanese artist and writer Gian Paolo
Lomazzo described in 1584 a terracotta bust of a Christ
Child supposedly by Leonardo, in his own collection.

The careful handling of the red chalk, more tonal
than *St James* (**57**) but less accomplished than the *Anghiari*
nudes (**78–82**), suggests a date around 1500. The putative
terracotta could thus have been executed either during
Leonardo's last years in Sforza Milan – perhaps for the
nursery of Ludovico's sons Massimiliano (b. 1493) and
Francesco (b. 1495) – or soon after his return to Florence.

64

The bust of the Madonna, c.1500

Metalpoint, red chalk, on pale red prepared paper.
22.1 × 15.9 cm. Melzi's *217*. R C I N 912514

The drawing is a study towards the so-called *Madonna of the Yarnwinder*, painted for the secretary to Louis XII of France, Florimond Robertet, whom Leonardo may have met in Milan in late 1499. The finest version (fig. 12) was probably executed by Leonardo in collaboration with assistants, as was common in Renaissance workshops. The drawing is some way from the painting in both pose and drapery, and the line of the back is particularly unsatisfactory.

Fra Pietro da Novellara, the Florentine agent of Isabella d'Este, Duchess of Mantua, saw a version of the painting in progress when he visited Leonardo's workshop in April 1501, hoping to persuade him to paint something for Isabella's collection:

> The little picture which he is doing is of a Madonna seated as if she were about to spin yarn. The Child has placed his foot on the basket of yarns and has grasped the yarnwinder and gazes attentively at the four spokes that are in the form of a cross. As if desirous of the cross he smiles and holds it firm, and is unwilling to yield it to his mother who seems to want to take it away from him.[13]

The painting thus combines a foreshadowing of the Passion, in Christ's seizing of the cross, with an allusion to the Madonna's forerunner, Eve, who was occasionally depicted spinning wool after the expulsion from Paradise – and so encompassing the Fall, mankind's subsequent travails, and our redemption through Christ's sacrifice.

F I G . 12
Leonardo and studio, *The Madonna of the Yarnwinder*,
c.1501. Oil on panel. 48.3 × 36.9 cm. By kind permission
of the Duke of Buccleuch & Queensberry KBE

65
Neptune, c.1504–5

Charcoal. 25.1 × 39.2 cm. RCIN 912570
(See also pp. 90–91)

This is a preparatory study for a highly finished drawing of the sea-god Neptune in his chariot drawn by sea-horses, described by Giorgio Vasari in his biography of Leonardo (1568) as drawn for Antonio Segni, an erudite collector and master of the Papal Mint. The finished *Neptune* is lost, and we have no certain record of it in a copy or print, though a drawing in Bergamo has been claimed as a partial copy.

The composition is an elongated oval, in the manner of an antique cameo or carved gem. Leonardo's inspiration may have been an ancient sarcophagus then at the church of Santa Maria in Aracoeli in Rome, showing Neptune standing in a low boat drawn by sea-horses placed either side of the god. Segni was in Florence until 1504, but the following April Leonardo was reimbursed for customs duty on a parcel of his clothes sent from Rome, and it is possible that he conceived the *Neptune* during a trip to Rome, during which he could have visited Segni and seen the sarcophagus at the Aracoeli. The tumult of man and horses is strongly reminiscent of the *Battle of Anghiari* (fig. 16), which Leonardo was developing at that time.

66 [OPPOSITE]
A horse and rider, and studies for Leda, c.1503–4

Black chalk, pen and ink. 28.7 × 40.5 cm.
Melzi's 26. RCIN 912337

In classical mythology, Leda, queen of Sparta, was seduced by Jupiter in the form of a swan and bore two eggs, from each of which hatched twins. Leonardo worked on two versions of a composition of *Leda and the Swan*, one in which Leda kneels, the other in which she stands. No patron or contemporary documents are known.

The kneeling composition (omitting the swan) is sketched three times on **66**, a sheet also containing a study of a horse and rider for the *Battle of Anghiari* (cf. **75**), and fully developed in two further drawings at Chatsworth and Rotterdam (fig. 13). Leonardo then abandoned the contrivance and instability of that format in favour of a more relaxed standing composition, which was copied by Raphael no later than 1508 (RCIN 912759). Over the next decade Leonardo executed a painting of the standing Leda that was still in his possession at his death in France, and five years later was the most highly valued item in the estate of his assistant and joint heir Salaì. The painting was in the French royal collection at Fontainebleau by 1625, but its ruinous state led to its destruction around 1700. Painted copies of the composition (fig. 14) agree in the main group but differ in the children and backgrounds; all however have a verdant setting echoing the fecundity of the main subject, and several of Leonardo's botanical drawings (see **105–110**) were probably made in connection with the painting.

FIG.13 [OPPOSITE, LEFT]
Leda and the Swan, c.1503–5.
Black chalk, pen and ink. 12.6 × 10.9 cm.
Rotterdam, Museum Boijmans Van Beuningen

FIG.14 [OPPOSITE, RIGHT]
Attributed to Cesare da Sesto, *Leda and the Swan,*
after Leonardo, c.1520. Oil on panel. 96.4 × 73.6 cm.
Salisbury, Wilton House, Collection of the
Earl of Pembroke

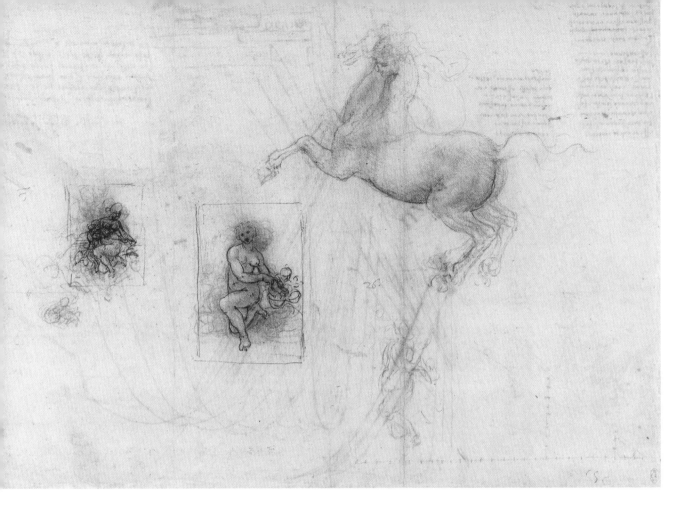

67
The head of Leda, c.1505–8

Black chalk, pen and ink. 17.7 × 14.7 cm.
Melzi's *12*. RCIN 912518

68
The head of Leda, c.1505–8

Black chalk, pen and ink. 20.0 × 16.2 cm.
Melzi's *11*. RCIN 912516

Drawings **67** and **68** are studies of Leda's head for the standing version. Leonardo expended little effort on her demure downward glance, devoting his attention instead to the most complicated of hairstyles: in **67** parallel plaits run over the top of her head, with a pattern of interlacing at the temples, while the principal study in **68**, with dense whorls over the ears, is the form on which Leonardo finally settled, as seen in most of the copies. Two smaller studies continue this coiffure at the back of Leda's head, with plaits woven into a dense criss-cross pattern (damaged by the acidic iron-gall ink eating into the paper). It was of course unnecessary for Leonardo to consider how the painted Leda's hair might look from behind; but a further study (RCIN 912515) carries a note – 'this kind can be taken off and put on without being damaged' – implying that he conceived Leda's hair as a wig, and that the drawings might even have had an ancillary function as studies for real wigs, perhaps for a festival or theatrical production.

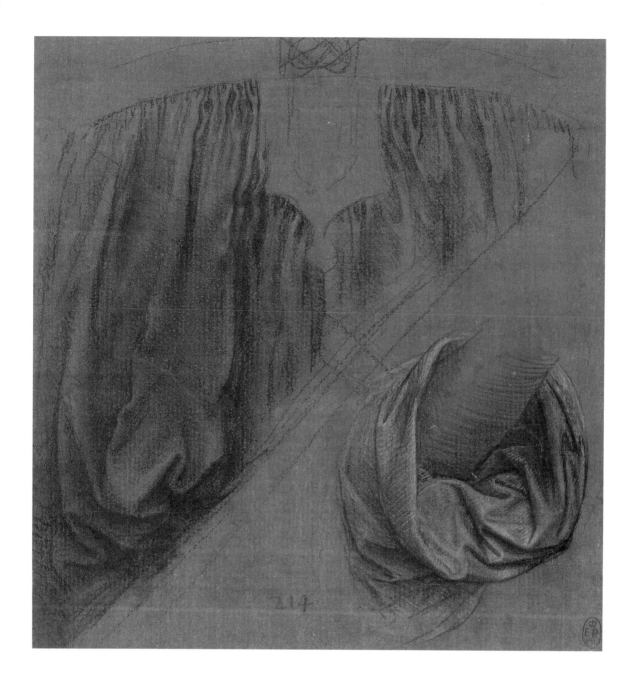

69
The drapery of a chest and sleeve,
c.1504–8

Red chalk, touches of black and white
chalks, some white heightening, on orange-
red prepared paper. 16.4 × 15.8 cm.
Melzi's 214. RCIN 912525

70
The drapery of a sleeve,
c.1504–8

Red chalk, touches of black and white
chalks, on orange-red prepared paper.
22.0 × 13.9 cm. Melzi's *218*. RCIN 912524

The drawings are studies for the drapery of the chest
and right arm of Leonardo's recently rediscovered
painting of Christ as saviour of the world, *Salvator Mundi*
(fig. 15). The subject would have been uncongenial to
Leonardo, a standard iconic formula that presented
little formal challenge or psychological tension. This
may be apparent in the unusually coarse handling of
the chalk, and the stiff lower drawing in **69** is probably
by an assistant, with white highlighting clearly by a
right-handed artist. But the areas of the painting that
survive in good condition are plainly by Leonardo,
not delegated to an assistant as in the *Madonna of the
Yarnwinder* (**64**), suggesting that the patron was both
important and discerning.

In 1504 the avid collector Isabella d'Este, Duchess of
Milan, wished to commission from Leonardo a 'youthful
Christ of around twelve years, of that age that he had
when he disputed in the Temple', but the *Salvator Mundi*
shows a mature, bearded Christ. Several copies of the
Salvator Mundi (and possibly the original) have an early
French provenance, and a commission from Louis XII
or his consort Anne of Brittany – who seem to have had
a particular devotion to Christ as Salvator Mundi – is
not improbable. The rich technique of the drawings
suggests a date around the middle of the first decade
of the sixteenth century, and the painting was perhaps
executed soon after Leonardo's return to French-
occupied Milan in 1506.

FIG.15
Christ as Salvator Mundi, c.1504–8.
Oil on panel. 65.5 × 45.1 cm.
Private Collection

The Battle of Anghiari

Leonardo's most ambitious painting – albeit unfinished – was the *Battle of Anghiari*, a mural intended to be perhaps 60 feet (18 m) wide, depicting a celebrated Florentine victory of 1440 over the forces of Visconti Milan. The painting was commissioned in 1503 by the Florentine government for the Great Council Chamber of the Palazzo della Signoria; the following year a counterpart, the *Battle of Cascina*, was commissioned from Leonardo's young rival Michelangelo. Though no record of the entire composition is known, Leonardo's painting was to show Milanese forces advancing from the left, a fierce cavalry skirmish at the centre, and, beyond a gulley spanned by a strategic bridge, the Florentine cavalry massing at the right.

In October 1503 Leonardo was given the use of a large room at Santa Maria Novella to prepare a full-sized cartoon. During 1504 and 1505 he was paid a steady salary, and the office of works of the Palazzo made payments for his assistants, for quantities of paper and paste for the cartoon, for painting materials and a movable scaffold, and so on. The painting was underway by June 1505 and proceeded until the summer of 1506, when Leonardo's temporary return to Milan was requested by the French occupiers of that city, and permitted by the Florentine government for diplomatic reasons. But there was growing ill-feeling between all parties, and Piero Soderini, leader of the Florentine government, complained to Charles d'Amboise, governor of Milan, that Leonardo 'has not conducted himself as he should have with the Republic, for he has taken a good sum of money and made only a small beginning to a great work that he should have done.'[14]

FIG.16
Peter Paul Rubens, *The Battle of Anghiari:
The Fight for the Standard*, after Leonardo, c.1612–15.
Black chalk, pen and ink, wash, white and grey
bodycolour. 45.2 × 63.7 cm. Paris, Louvre

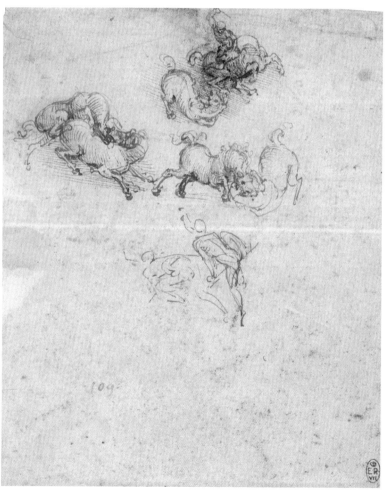

Although Leonardo was back in Florence at least twice in 1507 and 1508, he never resumed the painting. Only the central portion, known as the *Fight for the Standard*, was substantially completed (recorded in copies such as fig. 16), and this was obliterated – or, as has been claimed, concealed – after 1563.

Drawings **71** and **72** consider possible figures, horses and groups for the composition. The charcoal of **71** is heavily rubbed, but most of the motifs can be made out. From left to right we see a figure falling to the left while another lunges at him, brandishing a weapon aloft; a horse and rider galloping or leaping to the right; a rearing horse with rider, reminiscent of Leonardo's studies for equestrian monuments; two horses clashing, their heads twisted violently away, one rider holding a lance downwards; another study of two rearing horses with their riders trading blows, and a figure running to the left. Several of these motifs have the flavour of Paolo Uccello's three panels of the *Battle of San Romano*, the major Florentine precedent for a monumental battle scene.

The drawing in **72** is one of many small pen sketches for groups in the composition (others are in Venice, the British Museum and elsewhere), and emphasises that the horses were active participants in the battle. We see a rider raising his sword to strike a fallen horse (an unseated foe may be indicated at the centre of the group), and two ideas for horses fighting among themselves, kicking and biting. Two quickly sketched figures climbing over an obstacle link the sheet with the pen studies on **73**, the most diverse sheet for *Anghiari*, which includes men pole-vaulting across the gulley that would have separated the centre and right side of the composition, with further small sketches of standing warriors, and ten small studies of horses, galloping, rearing and kicking. The rearing horse at lower centre is copied from a Roman coin, and drawn alongside is the profile of Nero from the obverse of the same coin. Above, the note 'make a small one in wax, one finger long' must refer to a model of a horse or figure to aid Leonardo's development of the composition.

74
Galloping and kicking horses, and a foot soldier, c.1503–4

Red chalk. 16.8 × 24.0 cm. RCIN 912340

The largest study on the sheet, the half-length *Angel of the Annunciation* (**73**) in black chalk, is a feeble pupil's drawing, though Leonardo corrected the right arm with pen lines. A painting of the subject supposedly by Leonardo was stated by Giorgio Vasari in 1568 to be in the collection of Cosimo I de' Medici; no original is known, but of several versions by other hands, that in St Petersburg corresponds most closely with this drawing.

Although on a larger scale, the dynamic red-chalk studies of **74** are no more resolved than the pen sketches already discussed. The horse at full gallop, the cloak of its rider billowing in the wind, was intended for the left side of the composition; below is a smaller sketch of a galloping horse with its legs gathered beneath it. At upper left are three sketches of a foot soldier

75
A rearing horse, c.1503–4

Red chalk, pen and ink. 15.3 × 14.2 cm. Melzi's *112*. RCIN 912336

delivering a slashing blow with a sword, and at lower left an outline of a horse kicking, a memorable feature of Uccello's *San Romano* panel in the Uffizi.

Leonardo's sketches began to crystallise in more finished studies such as **75**, a rearing horse with its head thrown back in at least three positions, and the legs drawn repeatedly to give a sense of thrashing movement that echoes the contemporary *Neptune* (**65**). A jumble of lines indicates a rider, perhaps raising his right arm to strike a blow; below is a small faint pen sketch of a horse, its body again strongly twisted, as in so many sketches for the project. A list of Leonardo's books made around this time includes one 'of horses sketched for the cartoon', which presumably contained many similar studies.[15]

-112-

76
*A cavalcade, c.*1503–4

Black chalk. 16.0 × 19.7 cm. Melzi's *113*.
RCIN 912339

The group occupying the right side of the composition is seen in **76**, and it is striking that Leonardo should prepare such a huge mural with such small, meticulously worked studies. The Florentine cavalry is gathered on a low hill, preparing to join the fray, their standards fluttering above, while in the left distance a horse gallops away towards the bridge that was key to the battle.

77

A rearing horse, and heads of horses, a lion and a man, c.1503–4

Pen and ink, wash, a little red chalk.
19.6 × 30.8 cm. RCIN 912326
(Detail shown p. 100)

78 [FOLLOWING PAGES]

A standing male nude, c.1504–6

Red chalk, pen and ink, on red prepared paper.
23.6 × 14.6 cm. Melzi's *61*. RCIN 912594

79

A standing male nude, c.1504–6

Red chalk. 27.0 × 16.0 cm. RCIN 912596

The remaining drawings featured here are not directly preparatory for the composition, but 'background research' in which Leonardo sought deeper knowledge of the subject matter. On the right of **77** we see the horse of **75** again, but the rest of the sheet is given over to the expressions of fury in man, horse and lion, reflecting Leonardo's earlier note on the depiction of the vanquished in battle:

> Their brows raised and knit, and the skin above their brows furrowed with pain, the sides of the nose with wrinkles going in an arch from the nostrils to the eyes, the nostrils drawn up [...] the lips arched to show the upper teeth, and the teeth apart as if crying out in lamentation.[16]

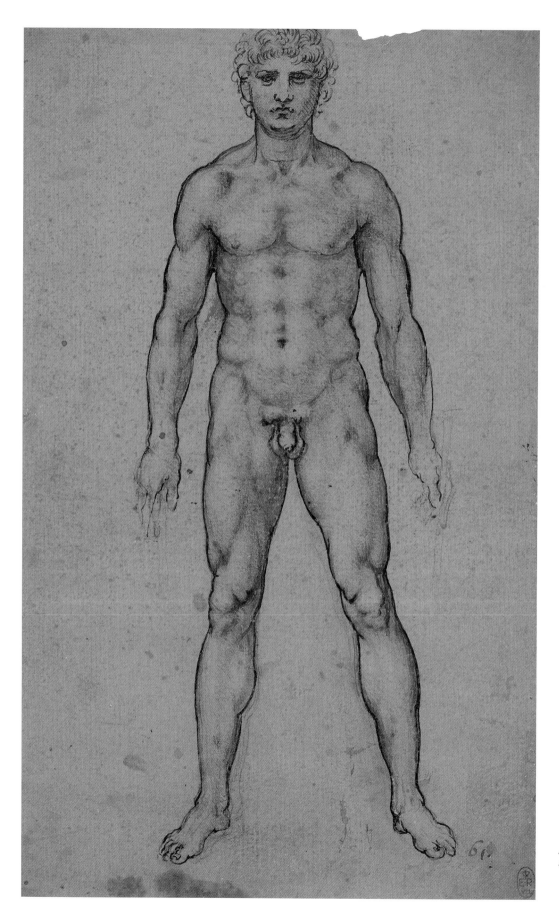

61.

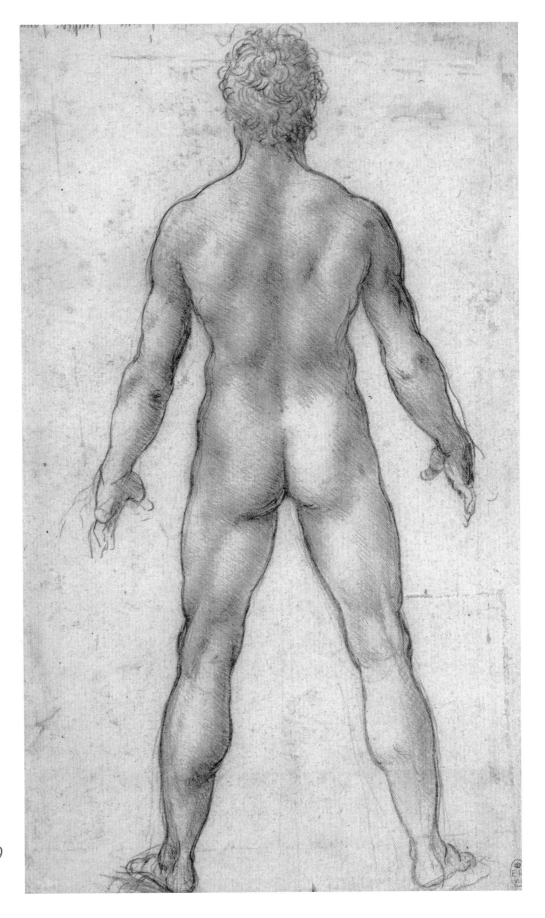

79

80

The legs of a male nude, c.1504–6

Black chalk. 22.3 × 14.0 cm. RCIN 912630

81 [OPPOSITE]

The legs of a male nude, c.1506–8

Red chalk, pen and ink, on orange-red prepared paper. 15.8 × 16.6 cm. Melzi's *73*. RCIN 912623

Leonardo returned to the study of anatomy in these years, to allow him to paint the monumental figures of *Anghiari* with complete confidence. Unlike his surveys of the human body around 1490 (**31–33**), there was now no attempt to derive a system of proportions: instead we see an empirical investigation of the appearance of the body, resulting in some of Leonardo's finest chalk studies. In **78– 79** the model spreads his legs equally to balance his weight distribution, and in **78** he supports his arms by holding sticks, so as to put no strain on the shoulder muscles. In **79** Leonardo strikes the perfect balance between subjective beauty and objective study of the underlying structures; but in drawings such as **80** he has perhaps been seduced by the possibilities of soft black chalk, for the depiction of light on skin has been achieved at the expense of the precise delineation of form, anticipating his late style (**172, 186**).

In **81** we see a model posed in the standard manner of figures in antique sarcophagi, with one leg flexed and the other extended straight behind. Such a figure seems to have been intended for the left side of *Anghiari* and may be prefigured by the swordsman in **74**, where the legs are reversed. The right leg shows individual muscles more distinctly than surface inspection of a living model can reveal, suggesting that Leonardo now had access to human corpses for dissection or flaying of the skin, by a medical collaborator if not (yet) by Leonardo himself.

The companion sheet **82** again shows the muscles of the legs, in several views, and then goes further to depict the bones of the pelvis and legs, with 'cords' indicating the lines of action of the muscles between

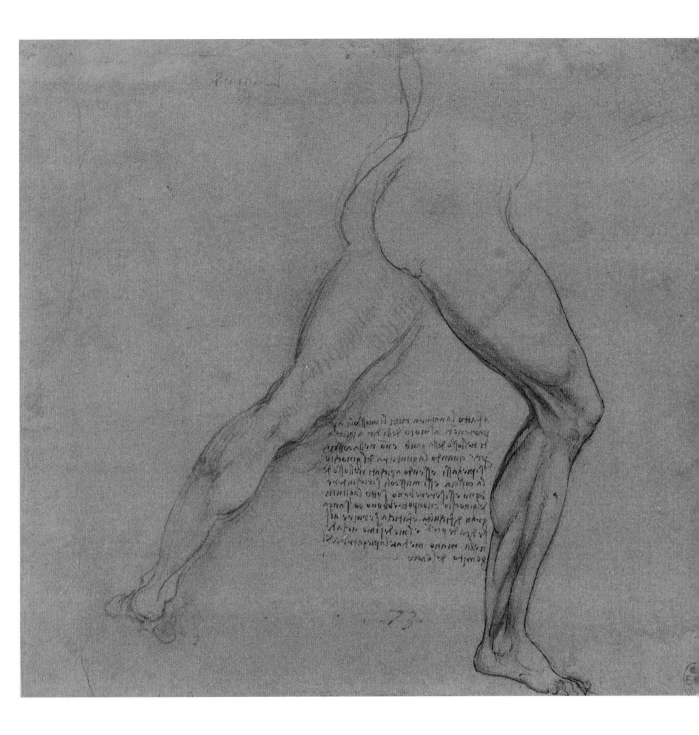

the pelvis and femur. Alongside two studies of human bones is a diagram of the same structures in the horse, with the astute note that 'to match the bone structure of a horse with that of a man you will have to draw the man on tip-toe'. A note referring to the Cordusio in Milan, and a Milanese watermark, indicate that the drawing was made after Leonardo had left Florence, and indeed the content of the drawing is now some way from the immediate requirements (if not the fundamental themes) of *Anghiari*.

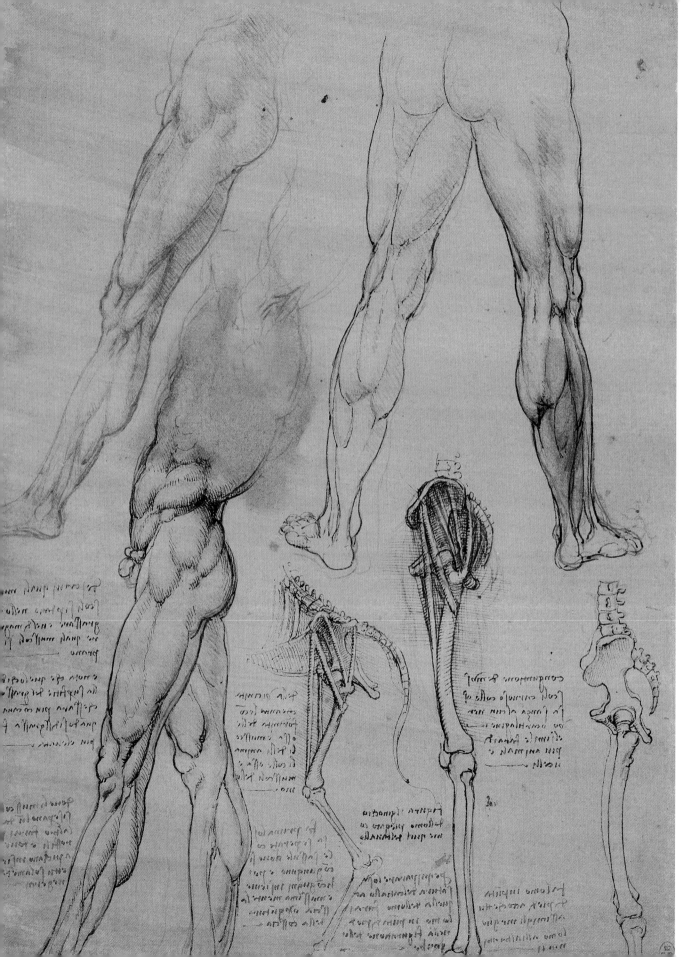

82

The leg muscles and bones of man and horse, c.1506–8

Red chalk, pen and ink, on orange-red prepared paper. 28.2 × 20.4 cm. RCIN 912625

83

The muscles of the shoulder, torso and leg, and a skirmish, c.1506–8

Red chalk, pen and ink. 16.1 × 15.3 cm. RCIN 912640

Illustrating this period of transition in Leonardo's priorities, the final sheet here, **83**, includes a careful little sketch of a skirmish, of a type familiar from the early studies for *Anghiari* (**72**, **73**), but now overshadowed by diagrams of the muscles. In three drawings the skin and right arm have been removed to show the muscles on the trunk and to analyse the actions of the individual shoulder muscles. In crude terms, Leonardo moved in his last decade from being a painter with scientific interests, to a scientist who painted a little when required, and sheets such as this stand on the watershed.

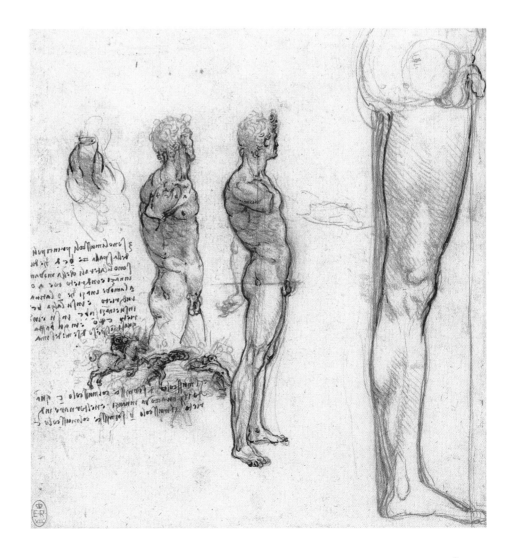

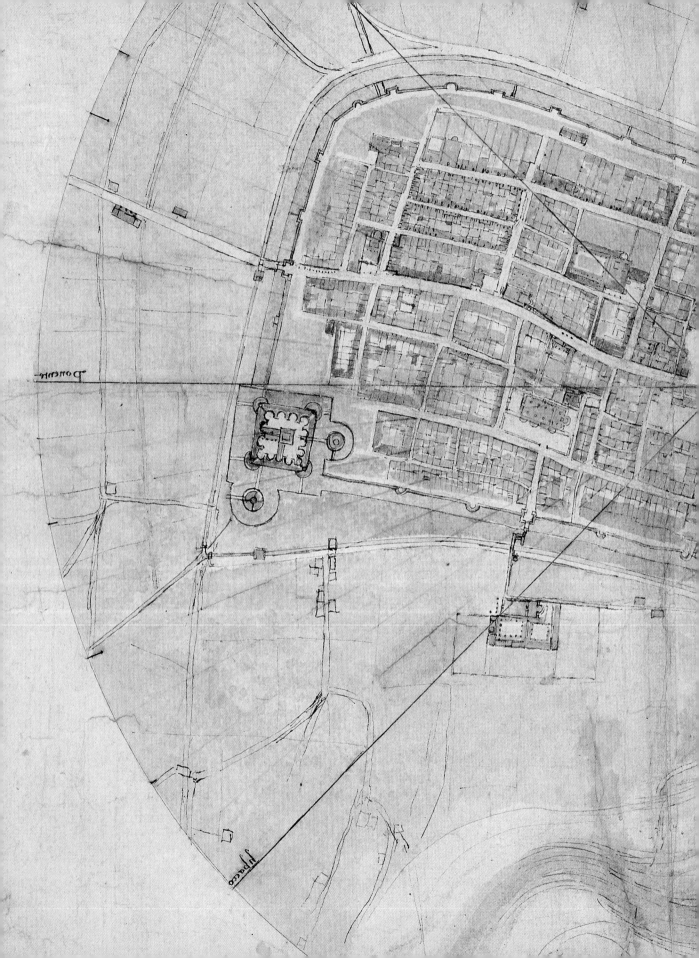

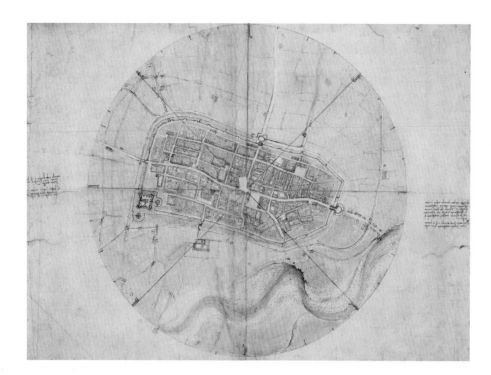

84

A map of Imola, 1502

Black chalk, stylus lines, pen and ink, coloured washes. 44.0 × 60.2 cm.
RCIN 912284
(Detail shown pp. 114–15)

In August 1502 Leonardo was appointed 'General Architect and Engineer' to Cesare Borgia, son of Pope Alexander VI and marshal of the papal troops, giving him powers to requisition men for surveying and to order improvements to fortifications. An alliance between the Pope and Louis XII of France in the late 1490s had led to Cesare being created duc de Valentinois and a lieutenant of the French army, and he possibly met Leonardo when the French invaded Milan in late 1499. Keen to assert his power in the Romagna – nominally part of the Papal States, but in effect a region of autonomous city-states – the Pope then ordered Cesare to march his forces south-east from Lombardy. Imola fell in December 1499, Forlì a month later, and Cesena, Faenza and Rimini the following summer.

Cesare lodged in Imola with his entourage in the autumn of 1502, and it must have been then that Leonardo made this magnificent map of the town. He paced the lengths of the streets, as recorded on an annotated sketch of each quarter of the town

(RCIN 912686), took bearings from the tower of the Palazzo Comunale at the central crossroads, and presumably worked out the layout by geometry on a lost sheet, as no construction lines are visible here (cf. **90**). The irregularities in the rectilinear street plan testify to the accuracy of the map, which may still be used to find one's way around Imola today. But it has been noted that some details of the buildings were out-of-date, suggesting that Leonardo relied on an earlier survey of the town for the ground plans and property boundaries – though why he or Cesare cared about such details is unknown, for their primary concern must have been the fortifications of the town.

Pen lines divide the circle into eight, each further sub-divided into eighths by stylus lines, allowing bearings to be given with some precision. In the margins Leonardo wrote the distances and directions to other towns and cities, such as 'Imola sees [*vede*] Bologna at five-eighths from the west towards the north-west at a distance of 20 miles [32 km].'

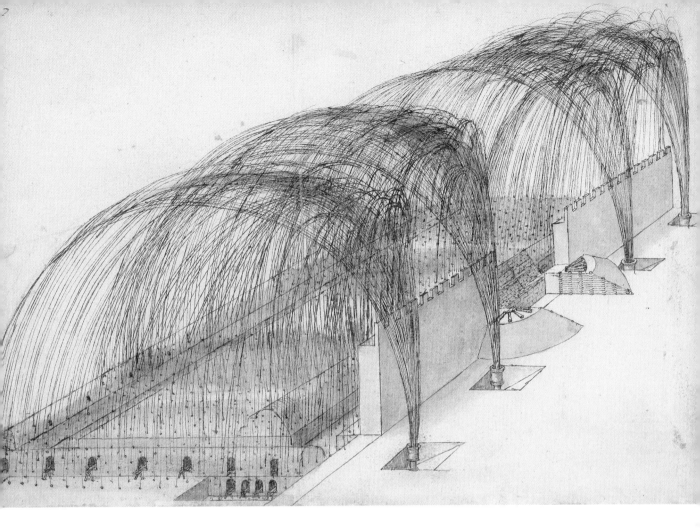

85
Mortars firing into a fortress, c.1503–4

Black chalk, pen and ink, wash.
32.9 × 48.0 cm. Melzi's *187*. RCIN 912275

This formal drawing shows how a fortress wall may be breached and the bailey within subdued. It deals with tactics rather than the design of a particular project, and suggests that Leonardo's earlier interest in military theory (**21–26**) was rekindled by his months spent surveying fortifications for Cesare Borgia.

Four mortars outside the walls rain stones into the fortress, where there are long covered galleries with gun emplacements. A section of wall has been undermined and has fallen into the inner ditch; cannon placed on earthworks either side of the breach, protected from assault by debris from the collapsed wall, direct their fire into the fortress. The vulnerability of the high medieval curtain wall following the introduction of gunpowder to European warfare in the fifteenth century led military architects to develop instead low, thick ramparts, with projections (bastions) to allow defensive fire in all directions, and increasingly elaborate systems of outworks.

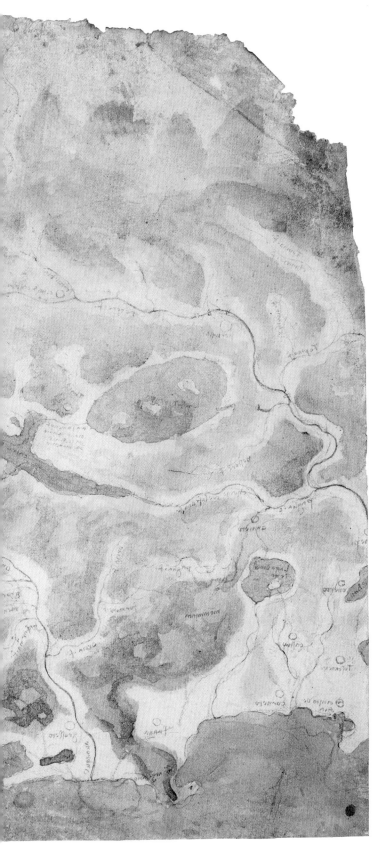

86

The rivers and mountains of central Italy, c.1502–4

Black chalk, pen and ink, brown and blue wash.
31.7 × 44.9 cm. Melzi's *175*. RCIN 912277

With north to the left, the map shows 170 miles
(275 km) of the western coast of Italy from La Spezia
to Civitavecchia, with the promontories of Piombino
and Monte Argentario heavily shaded. The focus of
attention is the Arno valley; the lakes of Valdichiana
and Trasimeno (see **89**) and the upper Tiber occupy the
right side of the sheet, and the Po is roughly sketched
at upper left, though it flows in the wrong direction.

Leonardo's drawing is based on a map of c.1470,
now in the Vatican but then in the ducal library in
Urbino, a city visited during his surveying work for
Cesare Borgia in 1502. Leonardo transformed his model
with the use of relief shading, and added much detail
in the upper Arno and its principal tributary the Sieve,
where mere streams and villages are included. This map
was relevant to several of Leonardo's projects in military
and civil engineering in the years around 1502–4, but
more generally reflects his long interest in the habits of
rivers. It is likely that he made it for his own reference
as a summary of all his available knowledge on the
topography of central Italy.

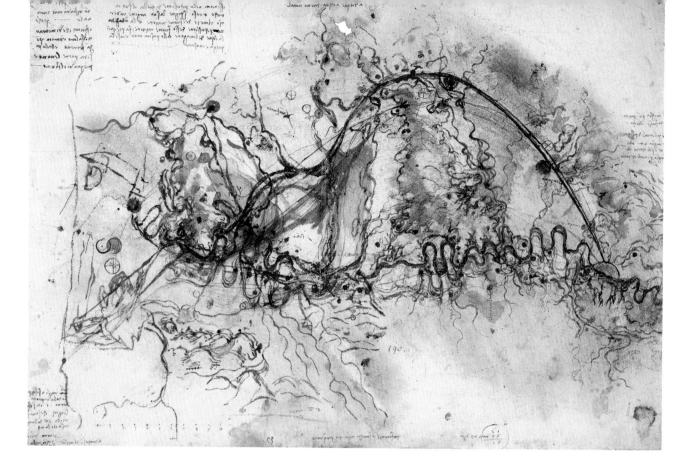

87

The Arno valley with the route of a proposed canal, c.1503–4

Charcoal, pen and ink, brush and ink, pricked through.
33.5 × 48.2 cm. RCIN 912279. (Detail shown pp. 8–9)

The Arno is not navigable as far as Florence due to rapids 10 miles (15 km) west of the city. A canal to bypass this stretch of the river had been suggested as early as 1347, and Leonardo enthusiastically promoted such a scheme around 1503–4. This vigorous drawing shows his proposed route for the canal: north from Florence via Prato and Pistoia, through a deep cut in the pass at Serravalle, into a marshy lake (seen in **86**), and then either rejoining the Arno at Fucecchio or passing into another marsh south-east of Lucca and thence into the Arno at Calcinaia. Leonardo hoped that the cities of Prato, Pistoia, Pisa and Lucca would contribute to the expense of digging and embanking the canal, as

all would benefit from the increase in trade, but there is no evidence that his plans were ever seriously considered by the Florentine government.

A second, unrelated scheme seems to be indicated at the left of the map. The Arno is not inked beyond the dark circle that represents Pisa, then under siege by Florence. Leonardo visited the Florentine camp in July 1503 and, with the support of Niccolò Machiavelli, proposed a scheme to divert the Arno and cut Pisa's access to the sea. Diversion channels seem to be drawn here as dark lines from the Arno south-west towards Livorno, and digging of a channel actually began in August 1504, but the scheme was soon abandoned.

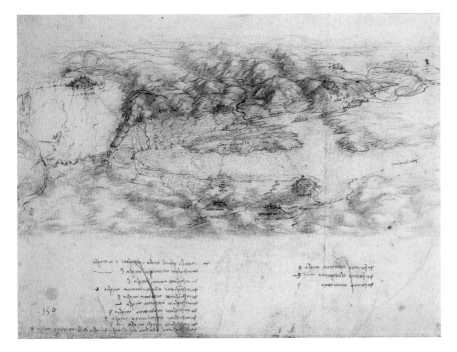

88

A bird's eye view of the Valdichiana, c.1503–6

Black chalk, pen and ink, wash.
20.9 × 28.1 cm. Melzi's *156*. RCIN 912682

89 [FOLLOWING PAGE]

A map of the Valdichiana, c.1503–6

Black chalk, pen and ink, wash, blue bodycolour. 33.8 × 48.8 cm. RCIN 912278
(Detail shown p. 13)

Leonardo's most pictorial map, **89**, centres on the long marshy lake that once occupied the Valdichiana in southern Tuscany. North is to the left; the Tiber runs along the top edge, and a bend of the Arno is at centre left; Perugia is at upper right, Arezzo at upper left and Siena lower centre. Leonardo presumably relied on a pre-existing map for the overall layout, but his measured sketch-map (in the Codex Atlanticus) of roads and streams around Castiglione and Montecchio shows that he surveyed at least some of the central area.

The drawing in **88** is an atmospheric bird's-eye view of part of the Valdichiana, with the hills receding to a misty horizon. Arezzo and the bend of the Arno are again to the left, and the lake of Trasimeno is in the right distance. Below, Leonardo listed and then crossed through the distances between Castiglione, Foiano and other towns in the vicinity, perhaps indicating that he used them when constructing **89** or some other map.

The purpose of the two sheets is not evident, though **89**, highly finished and with conventional script, must have been made for someone else to see. They have been associated with a revolt in Arezzo against Cesare Borgia in June 1502, or with Leonardo's plans for the Arno canal (**87**), which had involved damming the Valdichiana with sluices to feed the river and canal when low. But it is the lake of Valdichiana that is the focus of attention, and it seems likely that the maps were made in connection with a plan to drain the malarial marsh, a field in which Leonardo clearly attained some reputation (**95**). A channel cut northwards to the Arno in the fourteenth century to drain the lake had been only partly successful, and a channel cut in 1490 between Trasimeno and Valdichiana (seen in both maps here), to regulate the level of Trasimeno, had worsened the swampiness of Valdichiana. But no scheme is indicated here, and it was not until 50 years later that the digging of the present Canale Maestro along the length of the Valdichiana began in earnest.

90

A map of the Arno west of Florence, 1504

Stylus lines, pinpointing, black chalk, pen and ink.
41.0 × 25.7 cm. Melzi's *174*. RCIN 912677

91

A map of the Arno west of Florence, 1504

Pen and ink, blue and green wash.
42.2 × 24.2 cm. Melzi's *167*. RCIN 912678

During the summer of 1504 Leonardo surveyed
stretches of the Arno east and west of Florence, as seen
in several pages of sketches, measurements and records
of living expenses in the Codex Arundel (British Library).
From these surveys Leonardo constructed careful maps
of both areas – only **90** survives, dense with pinpoints
and stylus lines mostly invisible in reproduction – and
then traced them in 'fair copies', **91** and **92**, coloured
with green and blue washes and with notes written in
the conventional direction, identifying mills, the sizes
of sandbanks and so on.

The maps shown in **90–92** each cover about 2.5 miles
(4 km) of the Arno, with north to the left; the scale bar
on **92** is marked in units of 100 *braccia* (about 200 ft or
60 m), showing that the maps are drawn to a scale of
about 1:10,000. **90–91** cover the stretch from the Porta
al Prato, the western gate of Florence, to the village of
Peretola – the Arno has since been canalised through
this area, which is now occupied by the Parco delle
Cascine. **92** depicts the river to the east of Florence,
at the point where the railway now crosses the Arno.
Damage to the embankment is prominent at the centre
of the sheet where the river bends sharply, and further
downstream where the water gushing through a weir
strikes the bank. That area was depicted on a larger
scale in **93**, detailing the damage from the impact of the
current, and a second area of damage from the current
curving back into the riverbank.

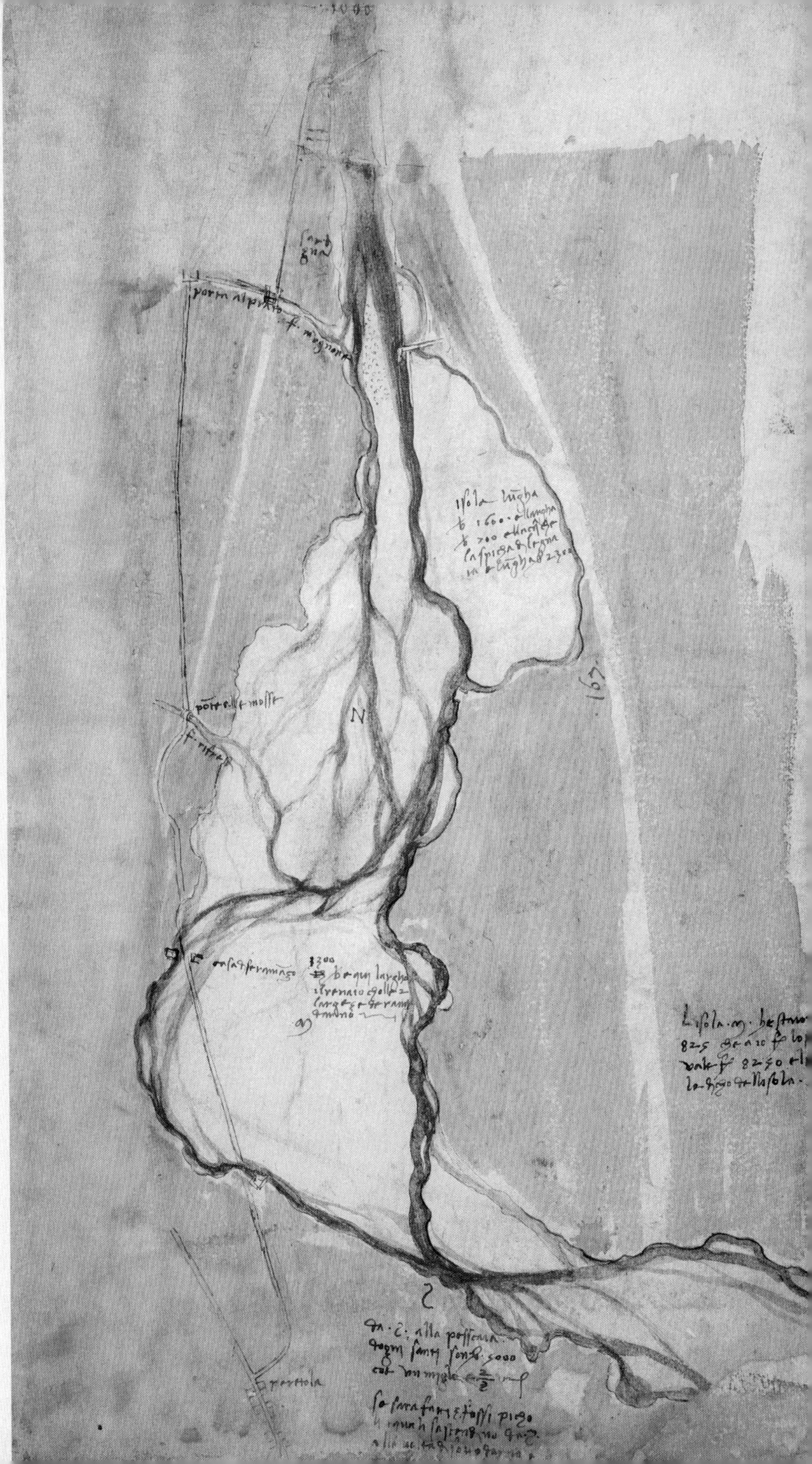

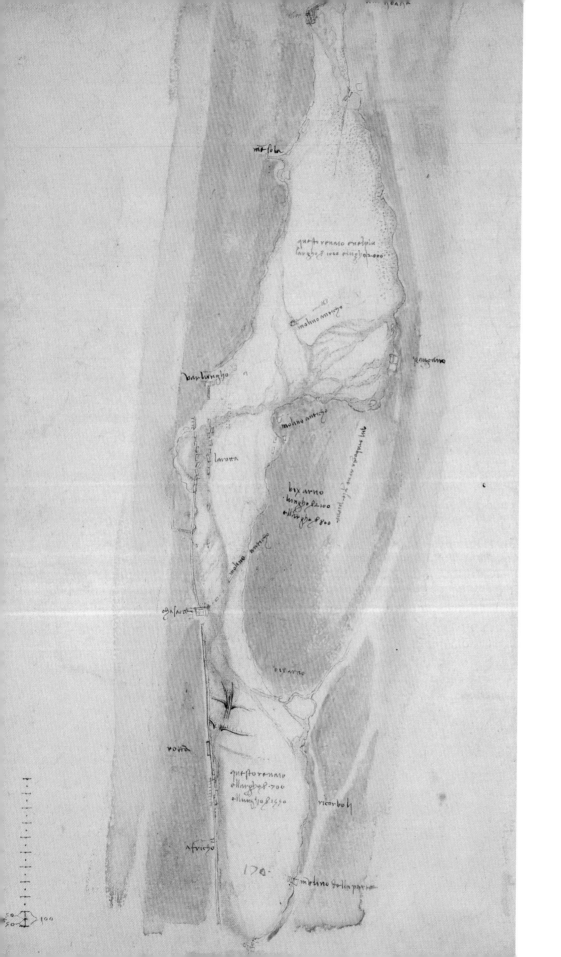

The notes and colour demonstrate that these were maps intended for others to see, and it has been suggested that the maps were drawn in connection with Leonardo's plans to construct a canal to bypass the Arno (**87**), which would have started around the centre of **90–91** and may also have entailed the canalisation of the river itself around Florence. More probably, the maps were commissioned from Leonardo by the city government: the Arno is a mountain torrent, low in the summer (which allowed Leonardo to survey its bed) but prone to flooding during the autumn rains and spring thaw, and the banks of the river required regular maintenance to keep its mills viable.

92 [OPPOSITE]

A map of the Arno east of Florence, 1504

Pen and ink, blue and green wash.
39.5 × 22.2 cm. Melzi's *170*.
RCIN 912679

93

A weir on the Arno east of Florence, 1504

Pen and ink, blue wash.
23.6 × 41.6 cm. Melzi's *168*.
RCIN 912680

94
A bird's-eye view of western Tuscany, c.1503–4

Black chalk, pen and ink, brown and red wash, blue
bodycolour (water damaged). 27.5 × 40.1 cm. RCIN 912683

The view is of western Tuscany as if hovering over
Chianti looking westwards, though the layout of the
towns is roughly correct in the plane of the paper with
no foreshortening of distances, and the drawing thus
functions as a map. About 80 miles (130 km) of coast is
shown; the Arno is to the right and the Cecina valley to
the left. Volterra is at lower left, Livorno on the coast at
upper centre, Pisa a little to the lower right, and Lucca
at the top right edge.

The map is rather old-fashioned by Leonardo's
standards, using the 'molehill' convention with towns
perched on the top of steep discrete hills and little

sense of the true topography of the area, and it is likely
that he was copying some pre-existing map. The area
depicted includes that relevant to the siege of Pisa
(see **87**), but there is no useful detail and Leonardo's
proposed diversion of the Arno is not shown. Similarly,
the right edge of the sheet shows portions of the lakes
through which his Arno canal would have reached
the river, but there is no hint that Leonardo had
that in mind when he made the map. Its purpose is
therefore unknown, though the colour and labelling
with conventional script indicate that it was made for
someone else to see.

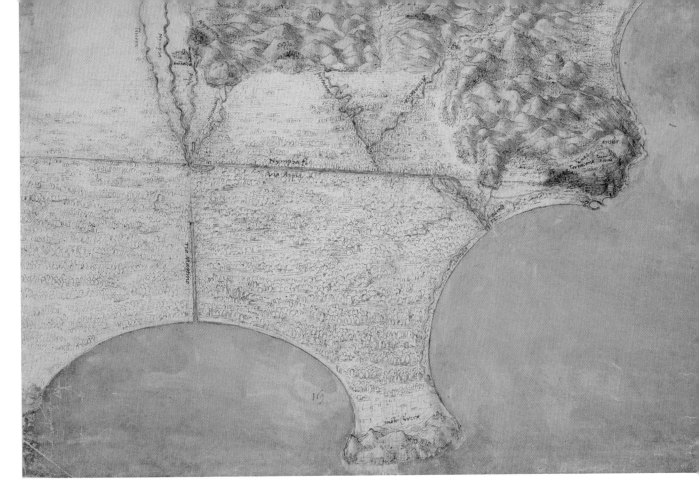

95
A map of the Pontine marshes, c.1514–15

Stylus, black chalk, pen and ink, brown and red wash,
blue bodycolour. 27.7 × 40.0 cm. Melzi's *169*. RCIN 912684

The map covers about 40 miles (65 km) of the coast south of Rome, with north to upper left, and depicts the plain of the Pontine marshes. Attempts had been made to drain these malarial marshes since Roman times, when the river Ninfa was canalised alongside the Via Appia (here passing horizontally to the coastal city of Terracina); around 1300 the Rio Martino (centre left) was dug from the Ninfa to the sea, but that soon silted up. In 1514 Pope Leo X charged his brother Giuliano de' Medici – Leonardo's patron in Rome – with draining the region, and a contract to carry out the work was signed by the engineer Fra Giovanni Scotti da Como in May 1515. This map demonstrates that Leonardo was involved in some capacity, though the drawing (with inscriptions by his pupil Francesco Melzi) was probably based on an earlier map, and Leonardo may not have visited the area himself.

The scheme was simple and is indicated with little fanfare: to clear the Rio Martino and reconnect it with the Ninfa; and to cut a new channel from the Ninfa to the sea, drawn as a diagonal line through the meandering rivers at centre right. Digging of that channel began in 1515, but the citizens of Terracina soon began to resent what they saw as papal annexation of their lands, and work halted with the deaths of Giuliano in 1516 and Leo X in 1521. It was not until the twentieth century that the marshes were fully drained and malaria eradicated, and the area still requires continuous pumping.

FIG.17
*Lisa Gherardini
('Mona Lisa'), c.1503–18.*
Oil on panel. 77 × 53 cm.
Paris, Louvre

96
A stand of trees, c.1500

Red chalk. 19.1 × 15.3 cm. Melzi's *127*.
RCIN 912431. (Detail shown pp. 130–31)

Leonardo had an instinctive response to the natural forces inherent in every landscape. His writings describe the interaction of water and rock with a profound sense of the vast timescales involved – the formation of rocks from sedimentary deposits, the uplift of mountain ranges, and the weathering of the mountains that returns their substance to the rivers and seas. He noted the presence of marine fossils in the mountains, and discussed how this evidence conflicted with the Biblical account of the Flood. These geological discourses were paralleled by the landscapes that signify timeless universality in several of his drawings and paintings – from some of his earliest known works, a drawing of 1473 (fig. 1) and his contribution to Verrocchio's *Baptism*, through the *Virgin of the Rocks* (fig. 7), to the *Mona Lisa* (fig. 17) and the late *St Anne* (fig. 19). And many notes towards his Treatise on Painting deal with the depiction of landscape – mountains, trees, clouds, rain and other atmospheric phenomena.

97 [OPPOSITE]
A storm over a valley, c.1506–10

Red chalk. 20.0 × 15.0 cm. Melzi's *137*.
RCIN 912409

In **96**, Leonardo drew a stand of trees at the edge of a wood with an almost miraculous range of touch, the red chalk sharpened to a point or used broadly, and occasionally wetted on the artist's tongue to add density in the shadows. This is a study of the effects of light on a mass of foliage, and a drawing of a single tree on the reverse of the sheet is accompanied by a note on the depiction of foliage in light or in shadow, relating both drawings directly to Leonardo's Treatise on Painting. There are similar studies of trees in Leonardo's notebook of *c*.1498–1502, with a note that could be taken to describe the present study:

> Trees: Small, lofty, straggling, thick foliage, dark, light, russet, branched at the top; some directed towards the eye, some downwards; with white stems; this transparent in the air, that not; some standing close together, some scattered.[17]

98
A mountainous landscape, c.1506–10

Red chalk. 8.7 × 15.1 cm. Melzi's *138*. RCIN 912406

The drawing in **97** depicts a storm in the foothills of the Alps, with the distant peaks sunlit above the storm clouds. Leonardo did journey into the mountains beyond Milan, recording an ascent probably of Monte Rosa during which he witnessed the darkening of blue sky at high altitudes:

> This may be seen, as I saw it, by anyone going up Monbroso [*sic*], a peak of the Alps which divide France from Italy. [...] Snow seldom falls there, but only hail in the summer [...] and in the middle of July I found it very considerable; and I saw the sky above me quite dark, and the sun as it fell on the mountain was far brighter than in the plains below, because less atmosphere lay between the mountain and the sun.[18]

Here, the tiny city in the plain and the rolling foreground hills are rather stylised; the drawing was most probably done in the studio rather than on the spot, and while it need not have been made while Leonardo was resident in Milan, the tendency to abstraction is compatible with his later years in that city.

The same simplification is seen in **98**, a tightly controlled depiction of an imaginary mountainous landscape. The jagged spires of rock rising from rounded hills are seen in the right background of the *St Anne* cartoon (fig. 18), to which the drawing is close in date, while the plain rising between the peaks to the right is reminiscent of the landscapes of *Mona Lisa* and the painted *St Anne*. The structure here is relatively simple, whereas in those late paintings the chains of mountains recede one after another until they are enveloped by

99
A mountainous landscape, c.1510–15

Black chalk. 8.8 × 14.5 cm. Melzi's *135*. RCIN 912407

the distant atmosphere: such depth is seen in **99**, in which the mountains rise indefinitely, growing larger the further away they are. The soft, grainy touch of the black chalk is closer in style to the *Deluges* (**190–196**) than to the *Storm* (**97**), and aims, like the *Deluges*, at poetic mystery rather than scientific precision.

Though similar in date, **100** is entirely different in character. Leonardo drew three separate sequences of mountains on the horizon, one above the other; at the centre are the peaks of the Grigne, near Lecco in the foothills of the Alps, as seen looking north from Milan – perhaps from the roof of the Duomo or a tower of the Castello Sforzesco. This is an extraordinary depiction of strong sunlight falling on mountains and seen at a distance through clear atmosphere. A companion sheet (RCIN 912414) bears a note on these effects:

The rocks of this mountain take on naturally a colour tending towards blue, and the intervening air makes them appear bluer still, particularly in the shadows. They also show dark marks from the minute trees which grow among them, and have in their dividing lines an ochre tone and violet-coloured marks. Outlines of a white tone are stone quarries, and among them are thick woods interspersed with meadows.

But Leonardo's drawings of such effects are monochrome, concentrating on the fall of light: he never attempted to capture in his drawings the colour effects described in his notes, despite his use of coloured washes in his maps (**86–95**).

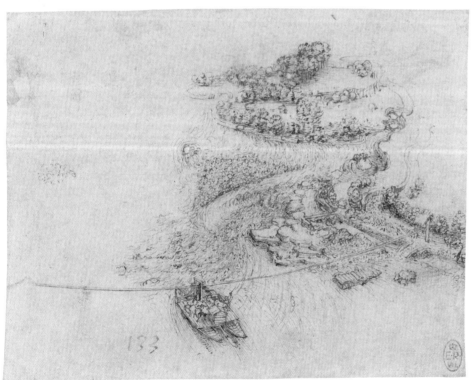

100

The Alps seen from Milan, c.1510–12

Red chalk, touches of white chalk, on orange-red prepared paper. 10.5 × 16.0 cm. Melzi's *181*. RCIN 912410

101

A river landscape, c.1511–13

Pen and ink. 10.0 × 12.8 cm. Melzi's *133*. RCIN 912400 (Detail shown p. 144)

102

A hillside with an outcrop
of stratified rock, c.1510–13

Black chalk, pen and ink. 18.5 × 26.8 cm.
Melzi's *161*. RCIN 912394

Leonardo drew his most exquisite landscapes while staying at the family villa of his pupil Francesco Melzi (see **152**), on the river Adda near Milan. **101** was drawn from the villa looking down into the valley, the Adda flowing towards us over a series of shallow rapids. In the foreground is a chain ferry, two hulls lashed together with a winching mechanism attached to a chain stretched from one bank to the other. On the ferry are several oxen and a herdsman raising a stick to strike one of the beasts, while another ox lumbers towards the landing stage. The drawing is tiny, and testifies to the precision of Leonardo's touch – and eyesight – even as he turned 60.

Such close observation is also seen in **102**, a hilltop with stratified rock bursting out of the ground and heaps of fragmented boulders in the right background. The perspective and scale, and the relationship between the parts of the drawing, are hard to grasp – the motifs seem to have been added individually without any overall compositional plan, a characteristic of drawings done in front of the subject. This effect is prominent in Leonardo's Arno landscape of 1473 (fig. 1), and some 40 years later we see here, at lower left, the same swirling, overlapping pen lines that serve little descriptive purpose, but are Leonardo's intuitive attempt to capture the invisible forces that bind the landscape together.

103
A rocky landscape,
c.1510–15

Black chalk. 16.4 × 20.1 cm.
Melzi's *182*. RCIN 912397

Leonardo's interest in rock formations was evident
as early as the 1480s, in the *Virgin of the Rocks* (see **20**).
Those rocks were ancient but stable, whereas in drawings from the last decade of his life they are subject
to massive forces that wrench them from the earth.
In **103**, slabs of weathered rocks are thrust upwards
and piled against each other, denuded of soil and
vegetation, while a torrent cascades over the strata at
lower left. A similar formation in reverse is seen in the
left background of the Louvre *St Anne* (fig. 19), and while
103 is probably not a direct study for that painting, the
connection emphasises Leonardo's understanding of
the earth as a place of infinite flux.

104

A rockfall in a mountainous landscape, c.1512–18

Black chalk. 17.8 × 27.8 cm.
Melzi's *188*. RCIN 912387

In **104** the side of the mountain is collapsing, great chunks of rock exploding outwards, issuing plumes and vortices of dust; what seems to be the entrance to a tunnel at lower right offers no protection from the forces of nature. This obsessive, terrible quality to Leonardo's late landscapes would reach its final expression in the *Deluges* (**188–197**), in which all matter is swept away.

Botanical studies

Leonardo drew plants and flowers throughout his life, following the tradition of naturalistic detail in fifteenth-century Italian art, of which Verrocchio's study of a lily (3) is a fine example. A drawing of *Venus and Cupid* for a tournament banner (*c*.1475; Florence, Uffizi) appears to be by Verrocchio in the figures and Leonardo in the carefully individuated plants, suggesting that the young Leonardo had a recognised interest in such matters. A list of drawings in his possession in the early 1480s includes 'many flowers portrayed from nature', and the first *Virgin of the Rocks* must have entailed such studies. Giorgio Vasari described in 1568 a cartoon by Leonardo of *Adam and Eve*, for a tapestry, including a 'meadow of endless kinds of herbage' and a fig-tree 'executed with such care that the brain turns at the mere thought of how a man could have such patience'.[19]

Leonardo's finest botanical drawings were executed in connection with his composition of *Leda and the Swan* (66–68). His compositional drawings for the kneeling *Leda* (fig. 13) and the painted copies of the standing version (fig. 14) all feature a verdant setting echoing the fecundity inherent in the myth. The paper and style of the botanical drawings most closely associated with the composition suggest that these were made in Milan after 1506, probably as work on the painting progressed.

The focus of 105 is a clump of star-of-Bethlehem (*Ornithogalum umbellatum* L.), whose swirling leaves are seen in the studies for the kneeling Leda and in most copies of the painting, where it softens the edge of the rock on which the swan stands (the same device is seen by the infant Baptist's legs in the *St Anne* cartoon, fig. 18, of a similar date). Flanking the star-of-Bethlehem is wood anemone (*Anemone nemorosa* L.), and below is sun spurge (*Euphorbia helioscopia* L.) with details of its seed-heads. Although the star-of-Bethlehem is somewhat stylised, the blades of grass growing untidily among and behind the anemones suggest that Leonardo observed these plants in the wild.

Also closely associated with *Leda* is 106, which depicts aquatic plants on both sides of the sheet – a branched bur-reed (*Sparganium erectum* L.), and on the reverse a bulrush (probably *Typha angustifolia* L.), prominent in the composition study (fig. 13). The seed-heads of the bur-reed are drawn with a precision far beyond the requirements of the painting: Leonardo was developing an interest in plant morphology as a subject in its own right, and studies such as these are more accurate than could be found in any contemporary herbal.

This red-on-red technique, combining fine detail and tonal subtlety, was used by Leonardo for many of his botanical studies. The drawing of oak (*Quercus robur* L.) and dyer's greenweed (*Genista tinctoria* L.), 107, displays a great variety of hatching in the backgrounds, the lines of chalk dancing around the plants and within the dense sprig of oak. A vertical fold in the sheet between the two drawings, and what seem to be stitch-holes in the fold, suggest that this is a trimmed folio from a sketchbook of plant studies. That sketchbook may also have been the origin of 108, a beautifully rendered study of guelder-rose (*Viburnum opulus* L.); the shape of the leaves and colour of the berries explain Leonardo's brief note 'maple, coral fruits'. The leaves are shown curling and sagging, for Leonardo was interested not merely in the shape of their outline, but also in their living form when subject to the natural forces of growth and gravity. The same is true of the studies of blackberry (*Rubus fruticosus* agg.), 109–110, a meticulously detailed drawing of a branch bending under the weight of its berries, and a detail of a side-branch together with a small study of bird's-foot trefoil (*Lotus corniculatus* L.).

105

A star-of-Bethlehem
and other plants, c.1506–12

Red chalk, pen and ink. 19.8 × 16.0 cm.
Melzi's *130*. RCIN 912424.

106

A branched bur-reed,
*c.*1506–12

Red chalk on orange-red prepared paper.
20.1 × 14.3 cm. Melzi's *126* (verso). RCIN 912430

A bullrush
Reverse of **106**

126.

107 [OPPOSITE]

*Sprigs of oak and dyer's
greenweed, c.1506–12*

Red chalk, touches of white chalk, on
orange-red prepared paper. 18.8 × 15.4 cm.
Melzi's *128* (verso). RCIN 912422

108

*A sprig of guelder-rose,
c.1506–12*

Red chalk, touches of white chalk, on
orange-red prepared paper. 14.4 × 14.3 cm.
RCIN 912421. (Detail shown p. 7)

109

A branch of blackberry,
c.1506–12

Red chalk, touches of white chalk,
on orange-red prepared paper.
15.5 × 16.2 cm. RCIN 912419

110 [OPPOSITE]

A branch of blackberry, and a
stem of bird's-foot trefoil, c.1506–12

Red chalk on orange-red prepared
paper. 18.8 × 16.5 cm. Melzi's *133*.
RCIN 912420

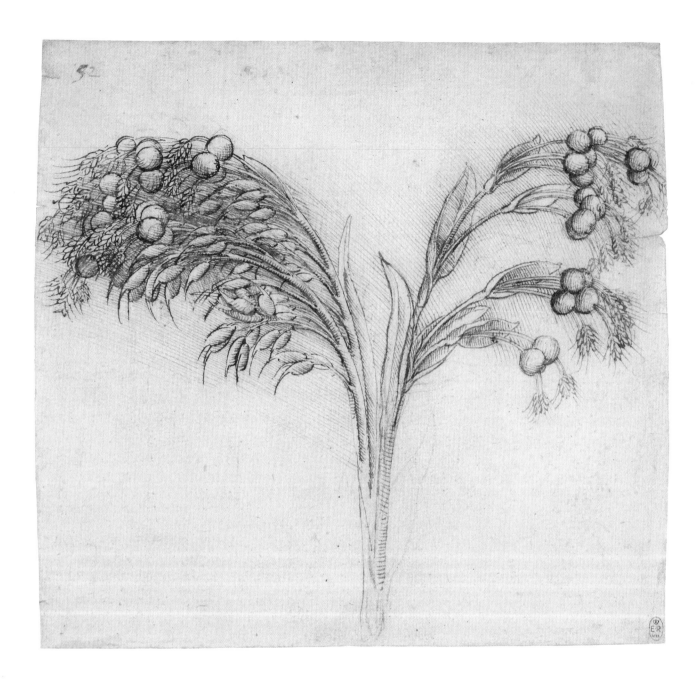

A few botanical drawings from this period cannot be associated with the *Leda* composition. **111** is a stem of Job's-tears (*Coix lacryma-jobi* L.), a grain-bearing grass native to Asia but now cultivated all over the world – this drawing is the first known record of the plant in western Europe. Leonardo clearly delighted in the contrasting forms of the seedheads, and the symmetrical arrangement on the page has suggested a connection with his designs for Villa Melzi around 1513 (see **152** and the reverse of **118**) or for Palazzo Medici in Florence around 1515, which included motifs of intertwined branches springing from trunk-columns. But such connections are thematic rather than direct: this is not an architectural study.

111 [OPPOSITE]

A stem of Job's-tears,
c.1510–15

Black chalk, pen and ink.
21.2 × 23.0 cm. Melzi's 152.
RCIN 912429

112

Studies of two sedges,
c.1510–15

Pen and ink. 19.5 × 14.5 cm.
Melzi's 153. RCIN 912427

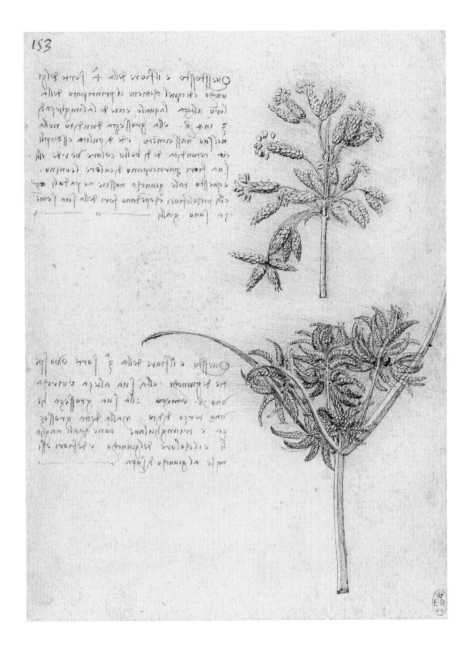

The last sheet here, **112**, is laid out more formally, two drawings of sedges – probably common club-rush (*Schoenoplectus lacustris* (L.) Palla) and nutgrass (*Cyperus rotundus* L.) – each accompanied by a block of descriptive notes. There are hints in Leonardo's notebooks of this period that he planned to compile a herbal, and the notes here are evidence of attempts at a system:

This is the flower of the fourth kind of rush, which is the tallest of them, growing three to four *braccia* [1.8–2.4 m] high, and near the ground it is one

finger thick. It is of clean and simple roundness and beautifully green, and its flowers are fawn-coloured. Such a rush grows in marshes and the small flowers which hang out of its seeds are yellow.

This is the flower of the third kind or species of rush, and its height is about one *braccio* [60 cm] and its thickness is one third of a finger. But this thickness is triangular, with equal angles, and the colour of the plant and the flowers is the same as in the rush above.

The Treatise on Painting and the Treatise on Water

Leonardo's return to Milan in 1506 saw a decisive shift in the emphasis of his activity. For the remainder of his life he was primarily a designer and scientist rather than a painter; and while he continued to work for many years on paintings such as the *Leda* (**66–68**) and *St Anne* (**154–159**), these were rarely the focus of his activity. His intended treatise on painting, begun 20 years earlier (see **30–33**), had spawned several distinct strands of investigation – anatomy, optics, water, atmospheric phenomena, the figure in motion and so on. Around 1508 Leonardo worked intensively on optics and water, and **113** is one of his most comprehensive sheets on the propagation of light and the casting of shadows. The sheet was compiled as four pages, one half inverted with respect to the other; the stooping man in red chalk is by a pupil.

Leonardo accepted the theory that light rays from an object consist of an infinite number of images of that object propagated in all directions, and at upper right he demonstrates that images can pass through a small aperture without interfering with one another.

At lower right he draws a camera obscura (the shaded box) with three objects and two apertures, giving two sets of three images on the inner surface of the camera. The diagrams below concern the optics of the eye: Leonardo knew that as light passes through the pupil the image must be inverted, but he assumed that the image on the retina is upright, and postulated that the lens must correct the direction of the image.

Other notes and diagrams examine the optics of illumination by multiple sources. At lower left Leonardo discusses the densities of shadows cast by a sphere illuminated by two extended light sources, while at upper left he examines the related phenomenon of coloured shadows of an object illuminated by differently coloured sources, in this case red and blue – as a painter Leonardo was interested in the colours of cast shadows and wrote extensively on the subject.

Small sketches at centre left show a sequence of a man striking the ground with a hammer, with the Latin heading *De pictura* ('On Painting') demonstrating that Leonardo was thinking specifically of his treatise.

113
Studies of optics and men in action, c.1508

Red chalk, pen and ink.
43.7 × 31.4 cm. RCIN 919149v

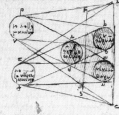
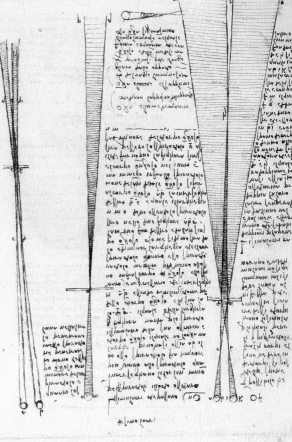

114

*Studies of men
in action, c.1508*

Black chalk, pen and ink.
20.1 × 13.0 cm. RCIN 912644

Many more such studies of men in action are seen on
114, one of a sequence of sheets containing about a
hundred such thumbnail sketches. Most of those are in
black chalk alone; here the chalk has been effaced, and
the pen line with which Leonardo fixed the outlines
is unusually hard and unattractive. Although there
is nothing systematic about these sketches, they are
symptomatic of Leonardo's constant desire to examine
every possible scenario, and elsewhere he enumerated
'the 18 actions of man: repose, movement, running,
standing, supported, sitting, leaning, kneeling, lying down,
suspended, carrying, being carried, thrusting, pulling,
striking, being struck, pressing down and lifting up'.[20]

Detail of **115**

115
Studies of water, c.1510–12

Black chalk, pen and ink. 29.0 x 20.2 cm.
RCIN 912660v. (Detail shown p. 153)

The movement of water haunts Leonardo's work in many fields. In his landscapes it is a symbol of natural processes over unconscionable timespans (**28**, **98–104**); in his civil engineering projects it is a powerful but tractable adversary (**87**, **89**); and in his scientific studies it is a pure element, responding perfectly to external forces in a manner that can be observed and analysed. Leonardo's work on water reached a peak during his years in Milan between 1506 and 1513, and several notebooks from that time, particularly the Codex Leicester, are rich with observations on the movement of water.

The drawing shown in **115** is the most masterly of Leonardo's drawings of the movement of water. The principal study shows the eddies and bubbles resulting from water falling from a sluice into a pool; the same topic is studied on **116** and **117** (the upper studies inverted), with each drawing recording a different pattern. They exemplify Leonardo's uncanny ability to fix a momentary impression in his mind and capture it on paper with absolute conviction, as if the endlessly changing scene had been frozen before him. But that visual lucidity collapsed when he tried to analyse the motions in words, for he lacked a satisfactory vocabulary to describe what he saw. Leonardo adapted terms from solid mechanics and optics, such as percussion, impetus and reflection, but his notes become increasingly opaque as he discusses the interactions of air and water, both striving to return to their original states:

> Water falling over other water, that water it hits and penetrates, but that part of it goes deeper which is farther from its extreme sides, and thus it reflects back with a welling motion, by which it returns to the surface, not as smoke does in penetrating through the air, but because of the bubbles or foam full of air it returns to the surface, urged by a double impetus, that is, the natural impetus of the air, and the impetus with which water moves such foam.

The upper two studies of **115** show the stable patterns of turbulence when a board is held at differing angles in fast-flowing water. A note considers the analogous scenario of the bow-wave of a ship, and how 'the water below the surface maintains the circumvoluted motion caused by its impact much longer than the water in contact with air. And this occurs because water within water has no weight, but it has weight within air.'

Studies of water, c.1510–12

Red chalk, pen and ink. 20.5 × 20.3 cm.
RCIN 912661

117
Studies of water,
c.1510–12

Red chalk, pen and ink.
26.8 × 18.2 cm. RCIN 912662

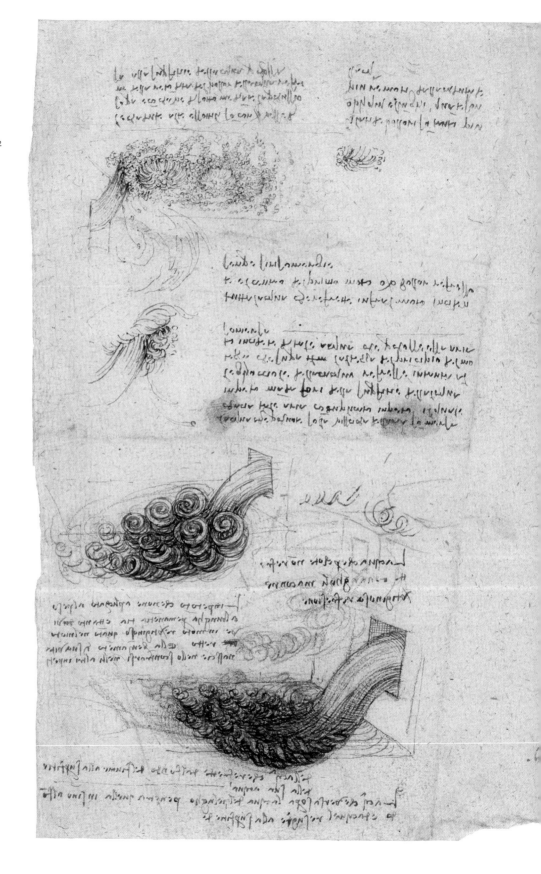

118

Studies of water, and a seated old man, c.1512–13

Pen and ink. 15.2 × 21.3 cm. Melzi's 57.
RCIN 912579. (Detail of reverse shown below)

The bearded old man seated on a rocky outcrop in **118** (occasionally claimed, whimsically, to be a self-portrait) appears to be gazing at the flows of water; but this is illusory, as the sheet was evidently folded when the drawings were made. The water studies again show a board held in flowing water, but they are more perfunctory than on the previous sheets, and were probably drawn from Leonardo's imagination rather than from observation. The distinctively coiling form of the water is explained by the note, 'observe the motion of the surface of the water which resembles that of hair, which has two motions, of which one depends on the weight of the hair, and the other on the direction of the curls.' Architectural studies on the reverse of the sheet are probably connected to Leonardo's work at Villa Melzi (see **152**).

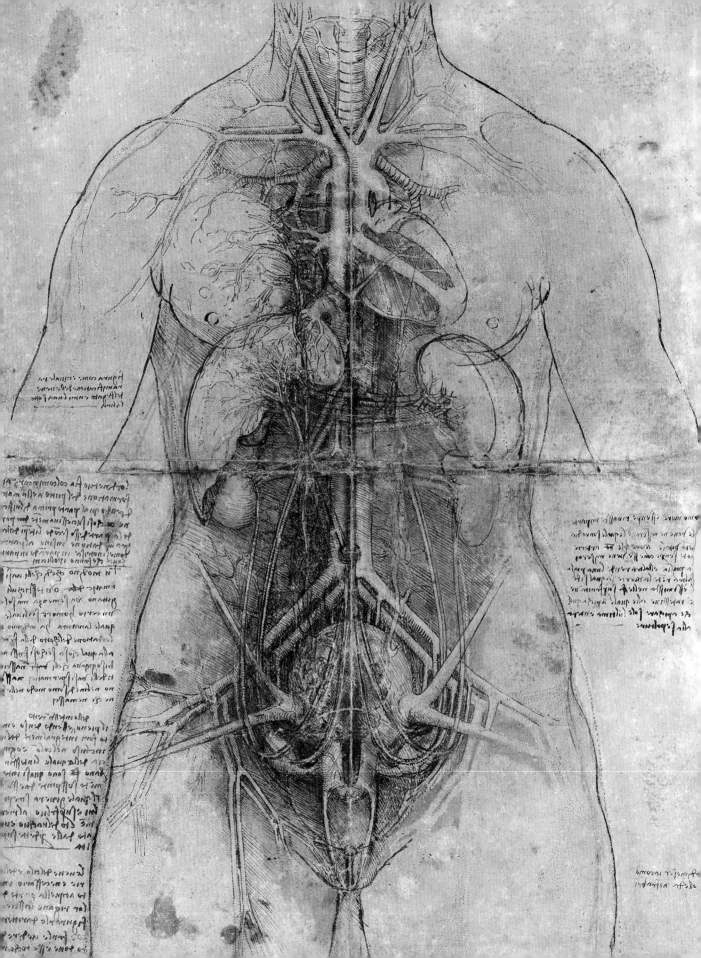

Late anatomy

By the end of his life Leonardo claimed to have performed 30 human dissections, but we have a description of only one of them, conducted probably during the winter of 1507–8:

> This old man, a few hours before his death, told me that he was over a hundred years old, and that he felt nothing wrong with his body other than weakness. And thus, while sitting on a bed in the hospital of Santa Maria Nuova in Florence, without any movement or sign of any distress, he passed from this life.
>
> And I dissected him to see the cause of so sweet a death, which I found to be a fainting away through lack of blood to the artery which nourishes the heart and the other parts below, which I found very dry, thin and withered. I performed this dissection very diligently and with great ease because of the absence of fat and humours which greatly hinder the recognition of the parts. The other dissection was of a child of two years, in which I found everything contrary to that of the old man.[21]

The subjects of human dissections at this time were usually executed criminals, or, as here, those who had died with no-one to claim their bodies for burial – the 'child of two years' mentioned above was presumably a foundling. The apparent ease with which Leonardo obtained permission to perform the dissections suggests that he now had some reputation as an anatomist, or at least that he was on good terms with physicians who facilitated his work. Over the next six years he made great advances in his understanding of human anatomy and physiology, and came close to completing the treatise that he had first envisaged during the 1480s (34–39).

119 [RIGHT]

The vessels of the liver, c.1508

Pen and ink. 19.1 × 13.5 cm. RCIN 919051v

Detail of **123**

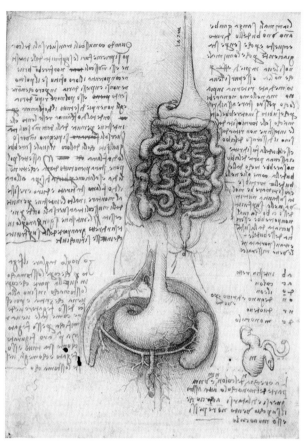

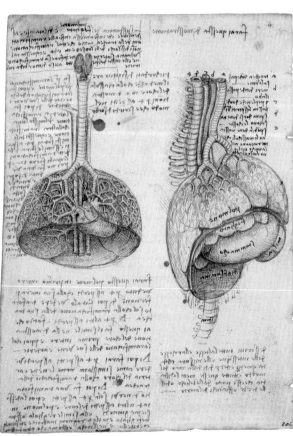

120

*The gastrointestinal tract, and
the stomach, liver and spleen, c.1508*

Black chalk, pen and ink. 19.2 x 13.8 cm. RCIN 919031v

121

The lungs, c.1508

Traces of black chalk, pen and ink.
19.4 × 14.2 cm. RCIN 919054v

Leonardo recorded his findings from the dissection of the old man in the notebook that he had used almost 20 years earlier for his skull studies (37–38). In **119** he depicts the vessels of the liver and their relationship to the aorta and vena cava, at centre left including the gall bladder, duodenum and outline of the stomach. It appears that the old man was suffering from cirrhosis of the liver and associated portal hypertension, and elsewhere in his notebook Leonardo gives the earliest known clinical description of that condition. In **120** the liver is shown in cross-section at lower left, with the hepatic portal vein curving below the stomach to the spleen. Above, Leonardo depicts the gastrointestinal tract; attached to the cecum, at the lower right (proper) of the intestines, is the appendix, seen again in the detail at lower right of the page – apparently the first description of this structure in Western medicine.

Though Leonardo now had access to human material, he still conducted animal dissections. The subject of **121** was a pig, commonly used for anatomical investigation through the ages, though Leonardo adjusted the proportions and orientation so that the lungs seem human at first glance. Leonardo conveys the branching of the bronchi by rendering the lungs semi-transparent; on the left he includes the heart, oesophagus and great vessels, and on the right, the liver, stomach and spleen nestling in the curve of the diaphragm, and the structures of the neck above – the trachea, oesophagus, carotids and vertebral column, with the long vertebral processes of a pig.

122

The uterus of a gravid cow, c.1508

Traces of black chalk, pen and ink.
19.2 × 14.2 cm. RCIN 919055r

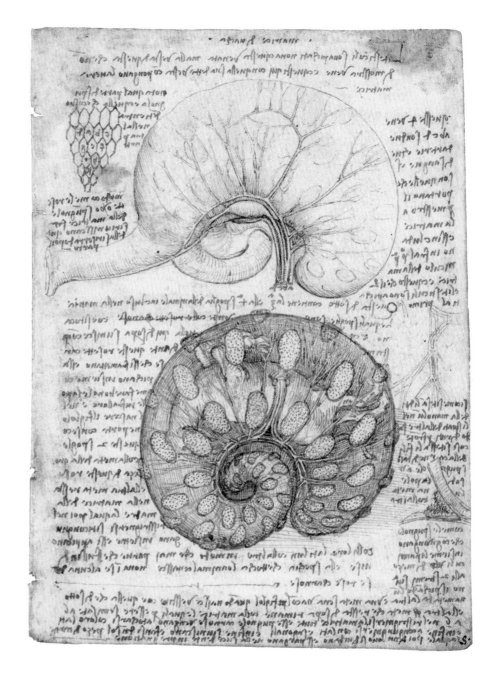

In **122** the animal subject is explicit, for the drawings show the two-chambered bovine uterus. In the lower study the uterine wall is removed to reveal a fetal calf in the upper chamber, on its back with its head to the left; Leonardo renders the chorionic membrane transparent, and the multiple bovine placenta as a pattern of small ovals. The upper study is an external view of the uterus, with an ovary at the centre and the vagina to the left. Though the page is headed 'uterus of the cow', the notes refer not to cow and calf but simply to mother (or animal) and infant: Leonardo assumed that all mammals have the same reproductive structures, and a few years later he applied to the human form the placental structure that he had observed in the cow (**139**).

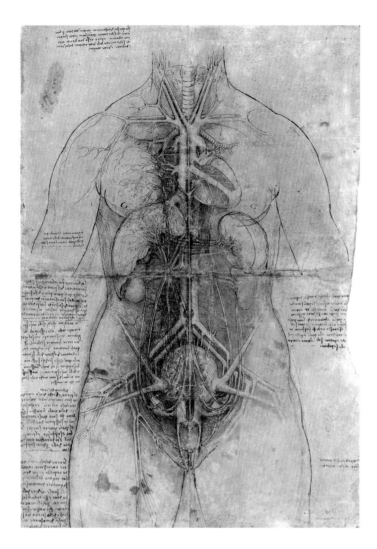

123
The cardiovascular system and principal organs of a woman, c.1509–10

Black and red chalk, pen and ink, yellow wash, on toned paper, pricked through.
47.6 × 33.2 cm. RCIN 912281
(Detail shown p. 158)

124 [OPPOSITE]
The brain, c.1508–9

Black chalk, pen and ink.
20.0 × 26.2 cm. RCIN 919127

This magnificent drawing summarises Leonardo's researches into the viscera following his dissection of the 'centenarian' (**119–120**). The great vessels are prominent down the centre of the sheet; the trachea and bronchi were transcribed from **121**, and the liver, spleen and kidneys from a companion sheet to **120**, though the gastrointestinal tract is not shown. The heart is drawn with only the ventricles and no atria. The ureters pass from the kidneys to the bladder, drawn as a circular outline over the vagina. The circular uterus is 'scalloped' within into seven chambers (following ancient tradition); the exaggerated uterine ligaments extending like horns to the flanks of the pelvis are probably derived from dissection of a cow (cf. **122**).

Leonardo clarified the spatial relationships of the organs and vessels by shading with pen hatching and yellow wash, and pricked through the outlines of the organs and vessels (the symmetrical elements by folding the sheet down the middle), to allow the sheet to be used as a template. He could then pounce chalk dust through the holes to make a pattern of dots to be joined with pen and ink, creating an unlimited number of 'clean copies' for further elaboration.

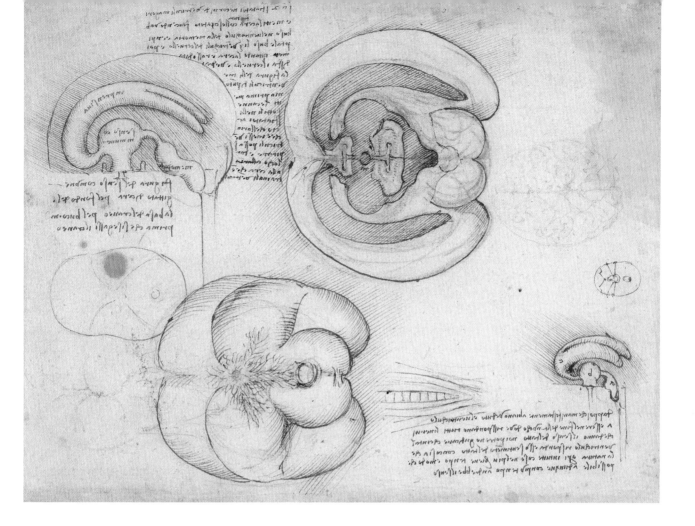

Leonardo's earlier anatomical studies adopted the traditional belief that the brain contains three bulbous ventricles arranged in a straight line (39). Even in later life, with more access to material for dissection, the softness of the brain and the difficulty of determining the shape of a cavity frustrated his attempts to determine the correct form of the ventricles. Adapting his knowledge of bronze casting, he therefore performed the procedure described in the note given at the top of 124:

> Make two vent-holes in the horns of the greater ventricles and insert molten wax with a syringe, making a hole in the ventricle of memory [the fourth ventricle, at lower right in each drawing]; and through this hole fill the three ventricles of the brain. Then when the wax has set, dissect off the brain and you will see the shape of the ventricles exactly. But first put fine tubes into the vent-holes so that the air which is in these ventricles is blown out and makes room for the wax which enters into the ventricles.

This is the first recorded instance in medical science of injecting a setting medium into a body cavity. The drawing at upper centre shows the brain cut in half through the mid-line and opened out; below is a depiction of the base of the brain. The other two studies show the three-dimensional form of the ventricles with reasonable accuracy, the lateral ventricles curving like horns to either side of the third (middle) ventricle, somewhat enlarged and distorted by the pressure of injection.

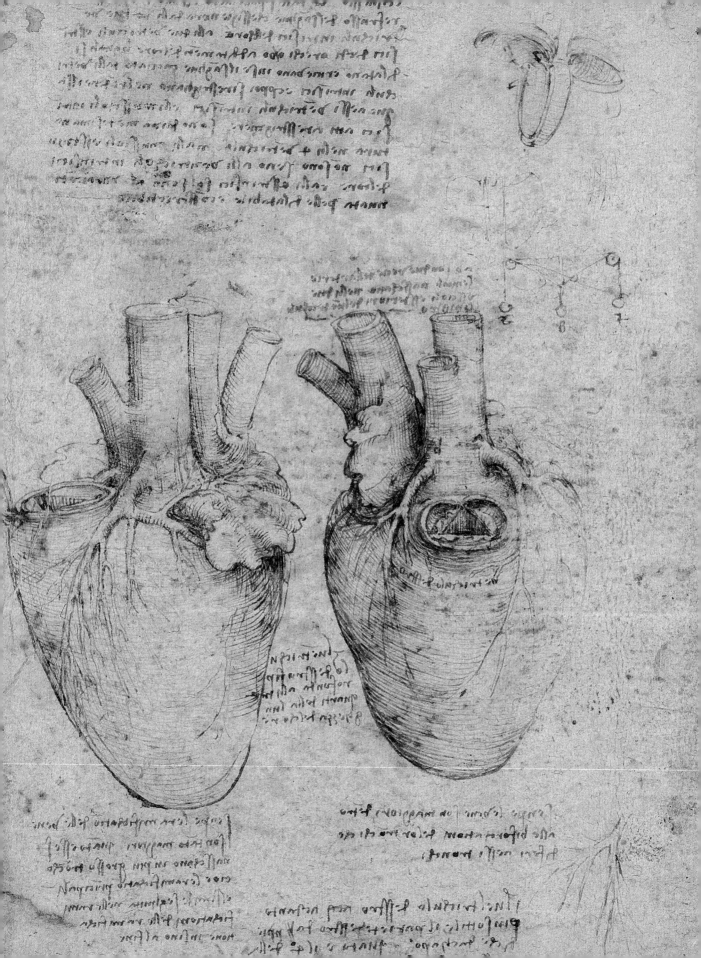

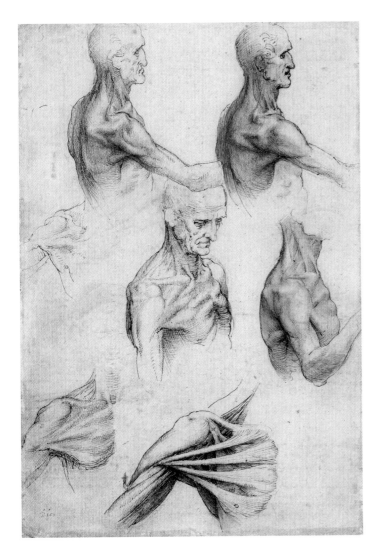

125
The superficial anatomy of the shoulder and neck, c.1510–11

Black chalk, pen and ink, wash.
28.9 × 19.8 cm. RCIN 919001v

In the winter of 1510–11 Leonardo was apparently working in the medical school of the University of Pavia, alongside the young professor of anatomy Marcantonio della Torre. He may have dissected up to 20 human bodies at that time, and recorded his findings on 18 sheets known as the Anatomical Manuscript A, crammed with more than 240 individual drawings and 13,000 words of notes. The bones and muscles were now the focus of Leonardo's investigations, rather than the internal organs, and on **131** he wrote that 'the book on the elements of mechanics [should] come before the demonstration of the movement and force of man and other animals; and by these means you will be able to prove all your propositions' – in other words, that all the body's actions can be explained by mechanical principles.

Working with a professional saved Leonardo from his tendency to get caught up in ever-finer detail. In these drawings he depicted every bone in the body except those of the skull (which he had portrayed brilliantly 20 years earlier, **37–38**) and most of the major muscle groups, and he developed novel illustrative techniques to convey the complexity of these mobile, layered, three-dimensional structures – orthogonal views in the manner of an architectural drawing (**132**), sequential views of a structure rotated in space (**127**), 'exploded views' (**133**), series of depictions of a structure gradually dissected (**128**) or built up (**131**).

The studies in **125** run as a sequence from upper right, turning the body in space to end with a frontal dissected view, which shows the chest muscle (pectoralis major) divided into four to emphasise its distinct portions and range of attachment. The sensitivity of surface modelling suggests that the drawings were made from the life, and the convincing manner in which Leonardo shows the skin stripped from tensed muscles in the last drawing emphasises his powers of visualisation.

Detail of **141**

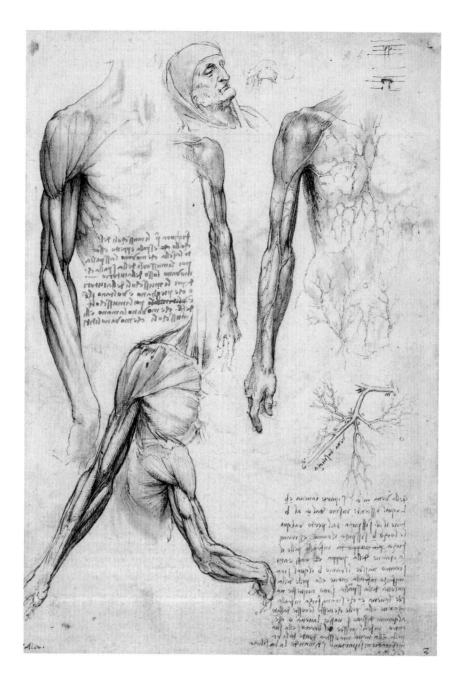

126

The muscles of the arm, and the veins of the arm and trunk, c.1510–11

Black chalk, pen and ink, wash.
28.9 × 19.9 cm. RCIN 919005r

127 [OPPOSITE]

The muscles of the shoulder, arm and neck, c.1510–11

Black chalk, pen and ink, wash.
28.8 × 20.2 cm. RCIN 919008v

The elderly and apparently dead man depicted at the top of **126** was presumably the subject of one of Leonardo's dissections. But anatomical drawings of the period frequently depict the subject posed as if alive, even when in a state of extreme dissection, and the studies of the arm and shoulder down the left side of the page give the old man the musculature of Apollo. With dabs of wash Leonardo captured the shimmer of the deep fascia, the connective tissue surrounding the muscles. The drawings at upper centre and upper right depict the trunk and arms with the skin removed to show the cutaneous veins.

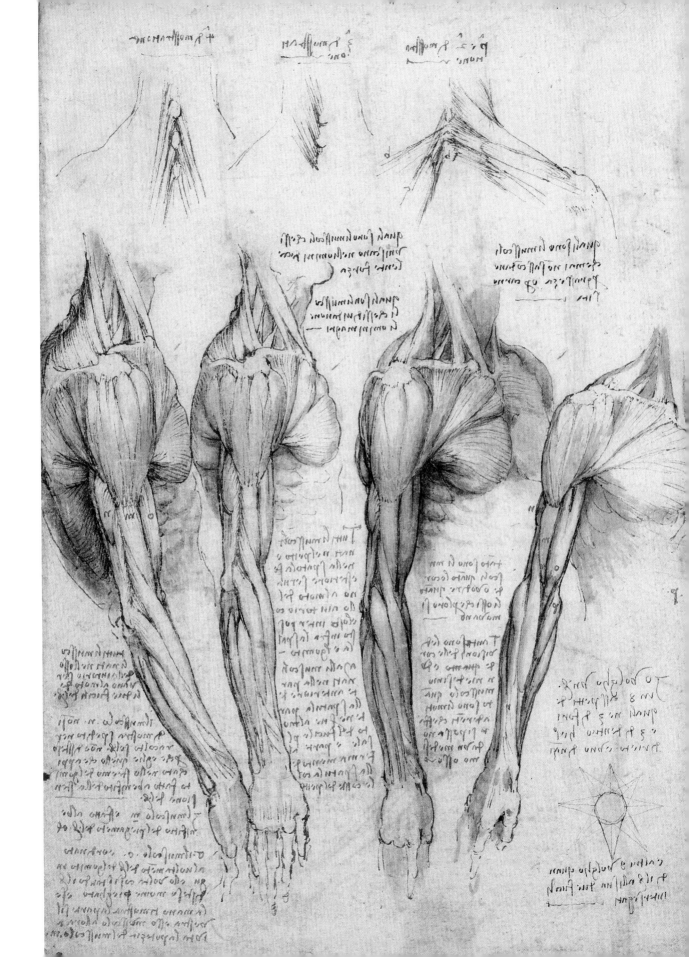

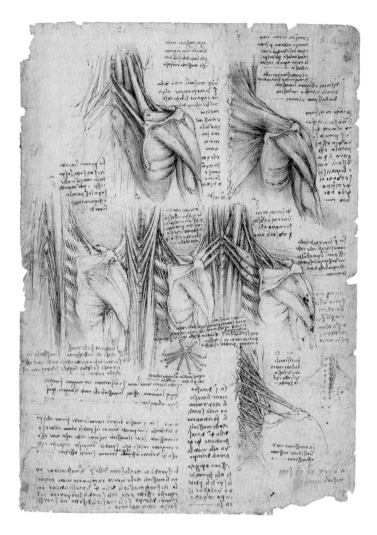

128
The muscles of the upper spine, *c.*1510–11

Black chalk, pen and ink, wash.
28.9 × 20.5 cm. RCIN 919015r

129 [OPPOSITE]
The muscles of the shoulder and arm, *and the bones of the foot, c.*1510–11

Black chalk, pen and ink, wash.
28.9 × 20.1 cm. RCIN 919013v

Leonardo was particularly fascinated by the shoulder, and in **127** he captures the spatial arrangement of the muscles by turning the body through 90 degrees (a sequence continued on the reverse of **126**, with a further four views from the back). Most of the superficial muscles can be identified, and the drawings and notes reveal a profound understanding of the region.

Three brief drawings at the top of **127** illustrate the muscles attached to the vertebrae of the neck, studied in much more detail on **128**. This is a finely layered region and difficult to dissect with fresh material; the five main studies of **128** are labelled *1st* to *5th*, showing a sequence of dissection from superficial to deep. At lower right is one of Leonardo's 'thread diagrams', combining the previous five drawings into a single schematic depiction, with each muscle represented by a cord along its line of action. Leonardo understood that

for almost every muscle acting on a vertebra, another acts in the opposite direction, both effecting movement and stabilising the spinal column.

A similar sequence of dissection views is found on **129**, in which the drawings at upper centre, centre and lower left are labelled *1st*, *2nd* and *3rd*. The first shows the superficial muscles; in the second the deltoid is lifted away to the left, and some of pectoralis major removed to reveal more of the shoulder joint; and in the third, pectoralis major is removed to the side of the humerus. At upper left is the shoulder from the side (less successfully), and at centre right is a small 'thread diagram' of the same aspect. In the larger study at centre right, the details of the neck and forearm are exquisitely drawn, especially the muscles and tendons that act upon the thumb. The study at lower right demonstrates the articulation of the ankle.

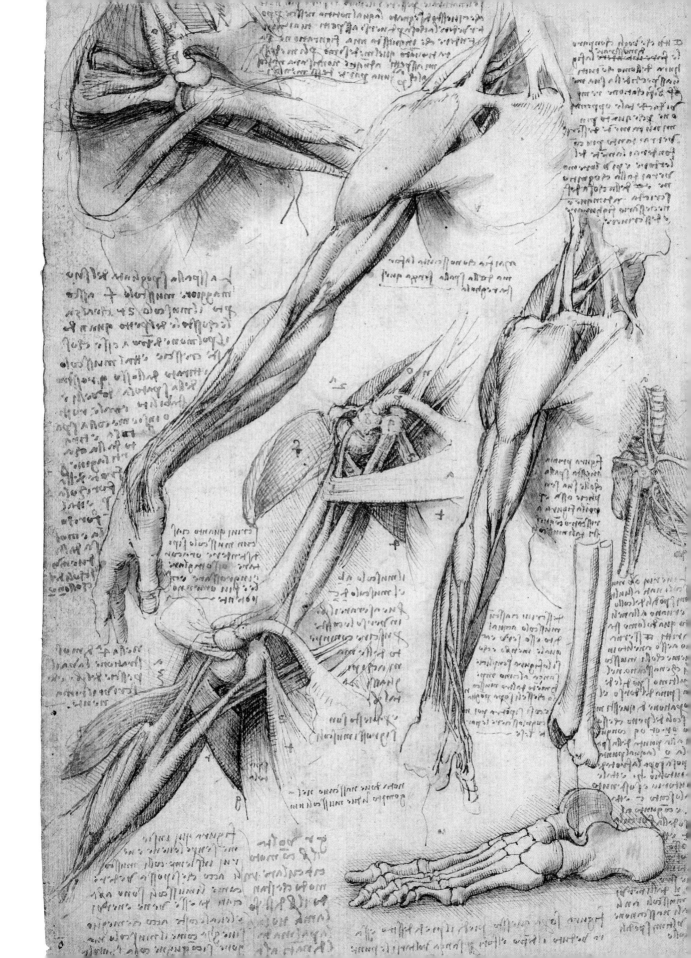

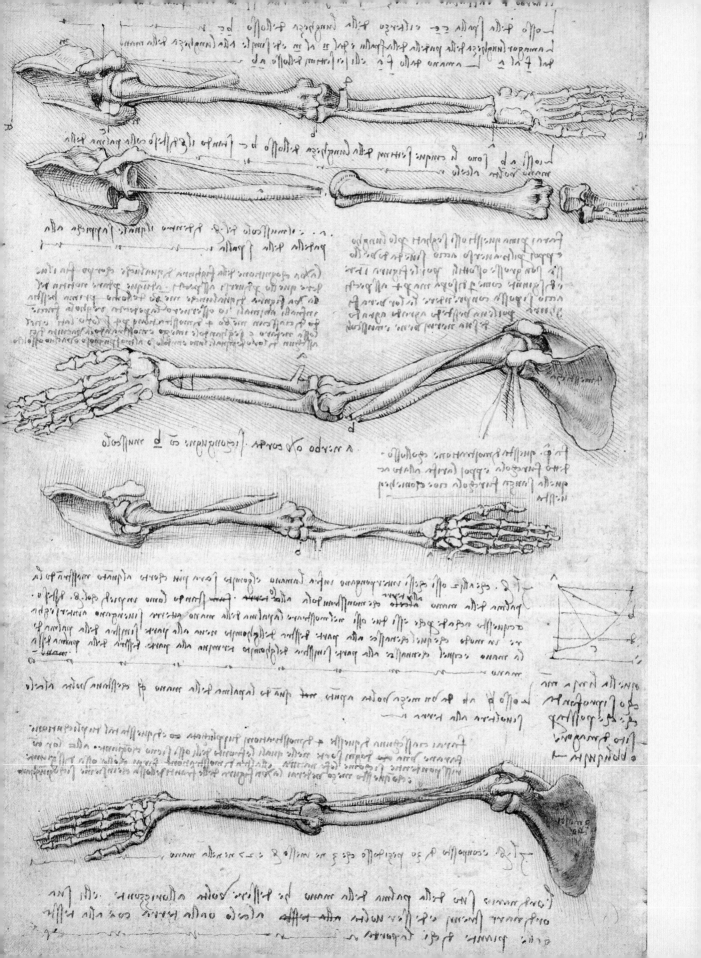

130 [OPPOSITE]

The bones and muscles
of the arm, c.1510–11

Black chalk, pen and ink, wash.
29.3 × 20.1 cm. RCIN 919000v

131

The bones, muscles and
tendons of the hand, c.1510–11

Black chalk, pen and ink, wash.
28.8 × 20.2 cm. RCIN 919009r

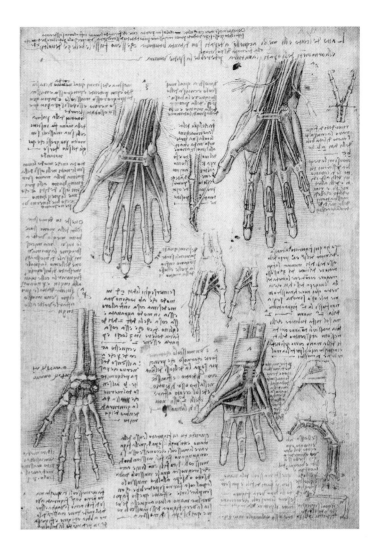

Leonardo's interest in the motions of the shoulder and arm continues on **130**, which investigates the rotation of the lower arm and hand. The upper two drawings show the arm and shoulder from above, first with the bones in their natural positions and then separated out to demonstrate their articulation. The only muscle shown is biceps, with its double origin on the shoulder blade (scapula): Leonardo discovered that biceps has two actions, both bending the arm at the elbow and rotating the forearm to turn the palm upwards (supination) – it would be two centuries before this observation was repeated. The lower drawings study the muscles in the forearm that turn the arm to direct the palm downwards (pronation).

In **131** Leonardo demonstrates the structure of the hand, building it up in the manner of an engineer. He begins at lower left with the bones, then adds the deep muscles of the palm and wrist at lower right, the first layer of flexor tendons at upper left, and the second layer of tendons at upper right. Leonardo was intrigued that the two sets of tendons bend the fingers in different ways, either with the finger held straight or curling the finger, as shown at bottom right; in each finger one tendon passes through a gap in the other, illustrated at upper centre, as he had observed in the bear's foot more than 20 years earlier (**36**).

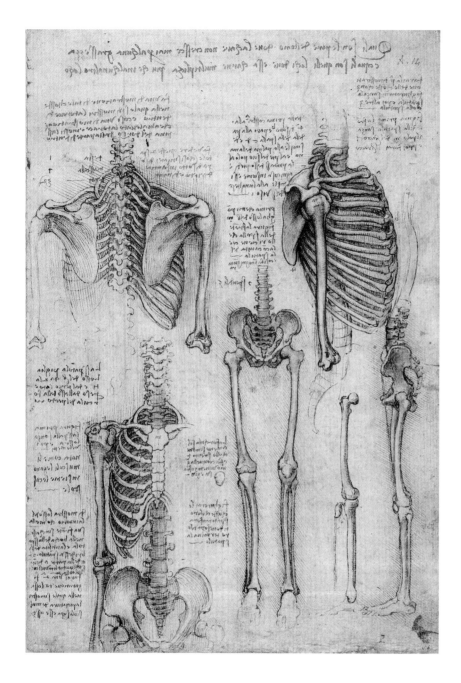

132

The skeleton, c.1510–11

Black chalk, pen and ink, wash.
28.8 × 20.0 cm. RCIN 919012r

133 [OPPOSITE]

The vertebral column,
c.1510–11

Black chalk, pen and ink, wash.
28.6 × 20.0 cm. RCIN 919007v

The drawing shown in **132** is Leonardo's most complete representation of a skeleton, seen from front, side and back. The studies at lower right show the line of action of the quadriceps muscle through the kneecap (patella). There are some errors of detail, such as the exaggerated length of the shoulder blade (scapula) against the ribcage, but the oblique placement of the ribs is well conveyed. And in **133** Leonardo achieved one of his greatest scientific drawings, the first accurate depiction of the spine in history, with its curvatures perfectly shown and the cervical, thoracic, lumbar, sacral and coccygeal sections correctly indicated. To the right is a frontal view of the spine, noting the variations in the sizes of the transverse processes (the spurs of bone to either side of the vertebral bodies). At lower left, alongside a view of the seven cervical vertebrae, Leonardo demonstrates how the first and second (atlas and axis) fit onto the third.

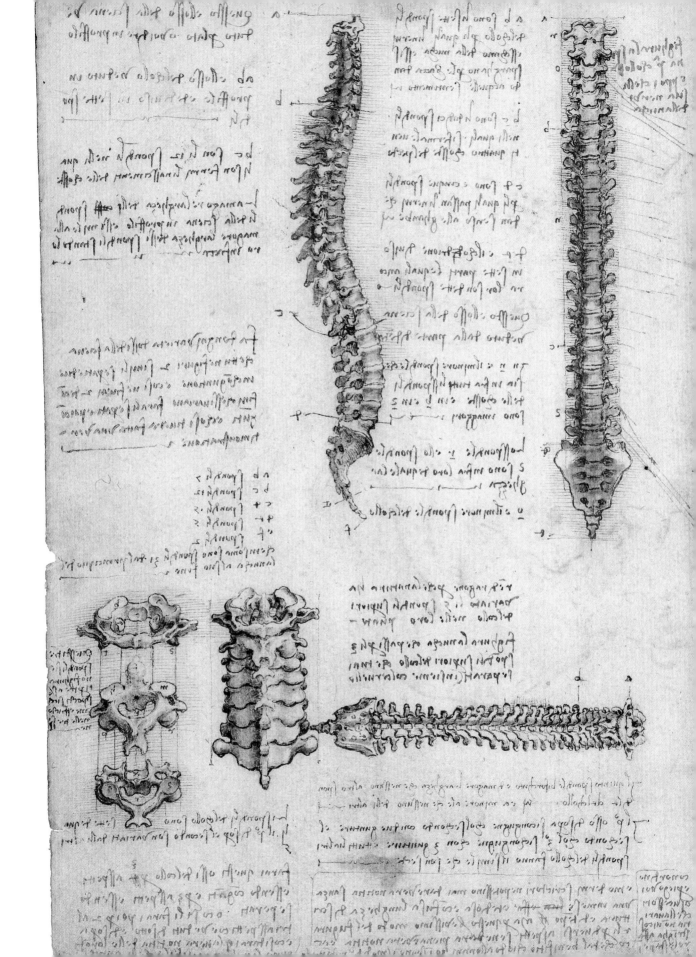

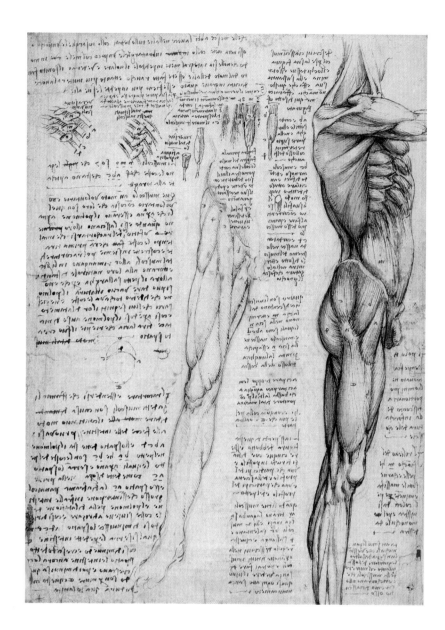

134
The muscles of the trunk and leg, c.1510–11

Black chalk, pen and ink, wash.
28.6 × 20.7 cm. RCIN 919014v

135 [OPPOSITE]
The throat, and the muscles of the leg, c.1510–11

Black chalk, pen and ink, wash.
29.0 × 19.6 cm. RCIN 919002r

The drawing in **134** is dominated by boldly modelled studies of the superficial muscles from the neck to the ankle. In the smaller diagrams and notes Leonardo analyses the structure of muscles in general – the mechanical function of the broad tendon of attachment, the muscle body, and the narrower tendon of insertion; the sensation due to the nerve; the 'nourishment' provided by the vein, and the 'spirit' by the artery.

Though the leg was presumably the first study on **135**, the remainder of the page is devoted to the throat, with drawings of the pharynx, larynx and trachea, and discussions of their functions in breathing, speaking and swallowing. The large drawings to the left display the uvula, the wishbone-shaped hyoid bone, the thyroid gland, and the thyroid, cricoid and tracheal cartilages; the odd form of some of the structures may have been derived from animal dissection. Individual features are studied in detail, such as the movement of the hyoid bone and epiglottis to prevent food or drink entering the airway of the larynx while swallowing.

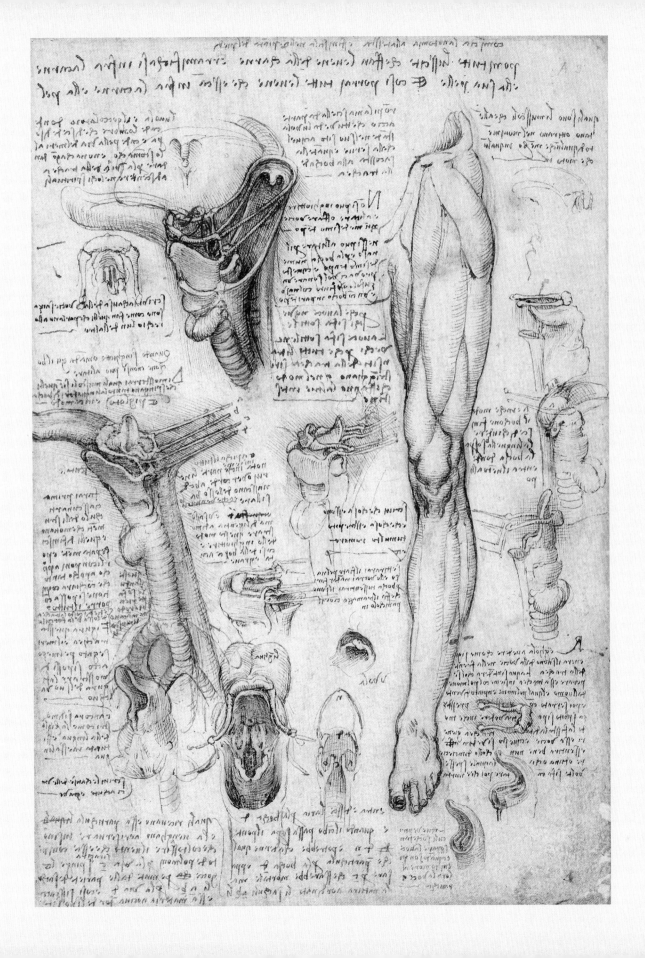

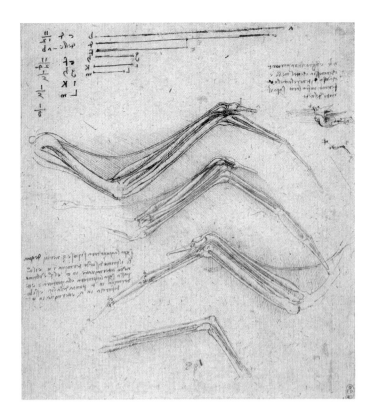

136 [OPPOSITE]

The muscles and tendons of the lower leg and foot, c.1510–11

Black chalk, pen and ink, wash.
38.9 × 28.2 cm. RCIN 919017r

The double-sized sheet **136** studies the muscles of the lower leg and the extensor tendons of the toes, on the top of the foot. In notes running to 1,200 words, Leonardo considers the physiology of contraction of the muscles and erection of the penis (both of which were believed to involve inflation with systemic air or 'pneuma'), and revisits themes treated throughout the manuscript – statements of intent to draw the bones separately from all sides, then joined, then with the muscles, then as threads to convey their layered structure, and so on.

Through the medium of a skilled engraver, the drawings of the Anatomical Manuscript A would have served magnificently as illustrations to the treatise on anatomy that Leonardo intended to publish, and on one of the sheets he states 'this winter of 1510 I believe I shall finish all this anatomy'. But the provisional nature of the notes is a reminder that, despite the high level of finish of the drawings, this was still a work in progress. The following year Marcantonio della Torre died of the plague; Leonardo lost his ready access to human material and the focus on completing the treatise that his collaborator seems to have encouraged, and his anatomical interests soon reverted to detailed studies of specific topics based largely on animal dissection.

137

The bones and muscles of a bird's wing, c.1512–13

Black chalk, pen and ink. 22.2 × 20.4 cm. RCIN 912656

For much of his career Leonardo dreamed of constructing a flying machine, but he had little understanding of aerodynamic lift, and assumed that a bird is kept aloft by upwards air currents or by flapping of the wings. The drawings here are dissection studies of the bones and muscles of a bird's right wing, probably intended to inform the designs of the flying machine. Despite their appearance, these are not 'thread diagrams': the muscles in a bird's wing are small, and used primarily for extending and retracting the light outer parts of the wing – Leonardo does not show the much larger breast muscle (pectoralis) responsible for powering flight.

In the right margin is a sketch of a bird in flight, the subject of Leonardo's entire notebook known as the Codex on the Flight of Birds (Turin, Biblioteca Reale). The anatomy of a bird's wing is also studied on **152**.

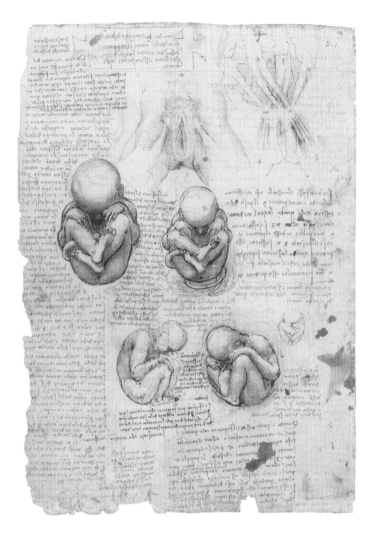

Throughout Leonardo's anatomical career he strove for objectivity, and colour is usually absent in his drawings towards the intended treatise. But in his late embryological sheets he used red chalk to evoke the coiled potential of the child in the womb, stepping back from the purely mechanical approach seen in the Anatomical Manuscript A (**125–136**) and returning to his early interest in the phenomena of life he noted on the drawing:

> In this child the heart does not beat and it does not breathe because it rests continually in water, and if it breathed it would drown. And breathing is not necessary because it is vivified and nourished by the life and food of the mother. … And one and the same soul governs these two bodies, and desires, fears and pains are common to this creature as to all other animated parts.

In both **138** and **139** the fetus is in breech position, with the umbilical cord wrapped around the crossed legs. Leonardo was puzzled that a fetus could fit into the uterus – he states that 'the length of a child when it is born is usually one *braccio* [*c*.60 cm]' but 'experience in the dead shows [the uterus] to be a quarter of a *braccio* in its greatest length'. He repeatedly drew the fetus curled up to occupy the smallest space possible, and in a note on **138** he compares the size of the human uterus with that of the cow and the horse, in proportion to their bodies.

In **139** the uterus is envisaged as if cut through and opened out, with an ovary in the left margin and the membranes in cross-section. Small sketches below show the uterine membranes unfurling like the petals of a flower. The placenta is shown throughout as multiple, a structure observed in Leonardo's earlier dissection of a cow (**122**) – though he seems to have dissected a pregnant woman at some point, he never discovered that the human placenta is single and discoidal.

138
The fetus, and the muscles attached to the pelvis, c.1511

Red and black chalks, pen and ink, wash.
30.4 × 21.3 cm. RCIN 919101r

139 [OPPOSITE]
The fetus in the womb, c.1511

Red chalk and traces of black chalk, pen and ink, wash. 30.4 × 22.0 cm. RCIN 919102r

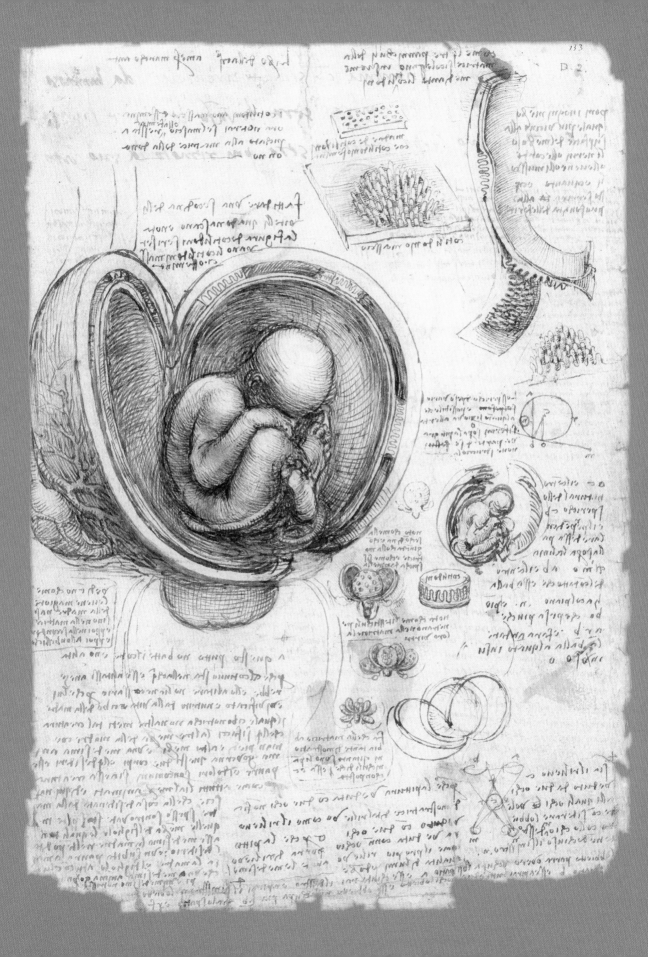

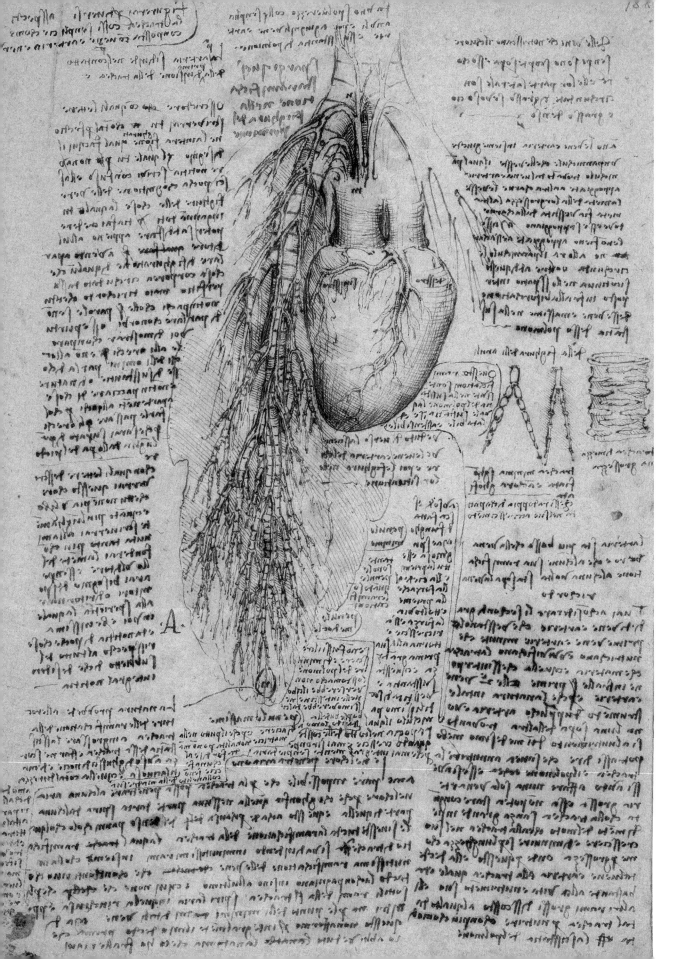

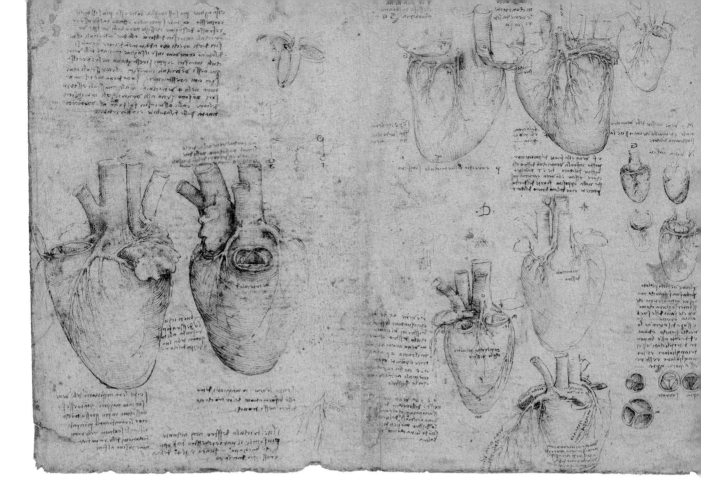

140 [OPPOSITE]

The heart, bronchi and bronchial vessels, c.1511–13

Pen and ink on blue paper.
28.8 × 20.3 cm. RCIN 919071r

Leonardo's last known anatomical campaign, his analysis of the heart, was perhaps the most brilliant of his many scientific investigations. A few years earlier he had satisfied himself that the heart (and not the liver) was the centre of the vascular system, and after 1511 he set about analysing the mechanics of the heart in a series of densely annotated sheets. Leonardo had little or no access to human material at this time, and his dissections were therefore of an ox's heart.

The drawing in **140** is a view of the heart, bronchi and bronchial vessels, with a description of the 'most minute' branching of the bronchi, accompanied by

141

The heart and coronary vessels, c.1511–13

Pen and ink on blue paper. 28.8 × 41.3 cm.
RCIN 919073v. (Detail shown p. 164)

veins and arteries 'in continuous contact right to the ends'. Leonardo refutes the traditional belief that air passes from the lungs directly into the heart (though he had no knowledge of gaseous exchange between the respirated air and the blood): 'To me it seems impossible that any air can penetrate into the heart through the trachea [i.e. bronchi], because if one inflates [the lung], no part of the air escapes from any part of it. [...] But I shall not wholly affirm this until I have seen the dissection which I have in hand.' That this refutation is both experimental and provisional demonstrates Leonardo's maturity as a scientist.

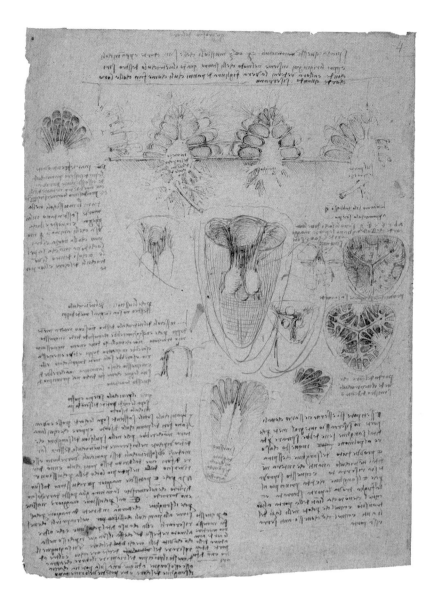

142
The right ventricle and tricuspid valve, c.1512–13

Pen and ink on blue paper.
28.4 × 20.9 cm. RCIN 919078v

The larger drawings on the double sheet **141** show several views of the heart with the aorta and superior and inferior vena cava, which in the ox merge before they reach the atrium. The pulmonary trunk has been removed to reveal the open pulmonary valve, while the coronary arteries leave the base of the aorta and pass to either side of the pulmonary valve. At lower right are small diagrams of a three-cusped valve, both open and closed: Leonardo intuited that the valves were key to the functioning of the heart.

At the centre of **142** Leonardo sectioned the right ventricle to reveal the papillary muscles within, their chordae tendineae (the 'heart strings') reaching up to the tricuspid valve. At centre right are two views, from either side, of the valve when closed. The diagram at the top of the sheet shows the heart cut through above and below the valve to give a rough cylinder, and then cut longitudinally and opened out. The three cusps of the valve are seen lying flat against the heart wall, with the papillary muscles along the lower margin and their chordae fanning out to the cusps.

143
The aortic valve,
c.1512–13

Pen and ink on blue paper.
28.3 × 20.4 cm. RCIN 919082r

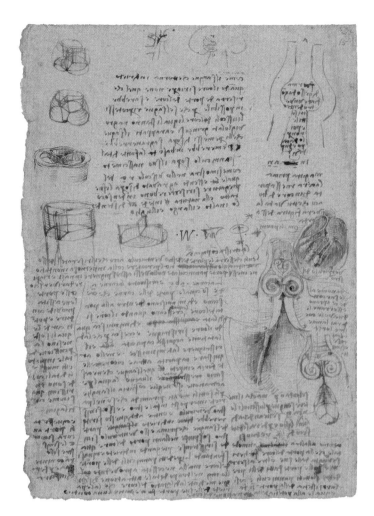

In an attempt to understand the flow of blood through the valves, Leonardo conducted a remarkable experiment, recorded on **143**, in which he poured molten wax into the cavities around the aortic valve (reprising his cast of the cerebral ventricles, **124**). From this wax cast he made 'a mould of gypsum for blowing thin glass inside' – in cross-section at top right – and then pumped water mixed with grass seeds through his glass model to study the flow patterns. He observed turbulent vortices in the widening (sinus) beyond the valve, drawn schematically at centre right, and correctly concluded that these vortices are responsible for opening out the cusps and closing the valve when blood flow ceases after each beat of the heart – otherwise, he surmised, reflux of the blood during diastole would cause the cusps to crumple and the valve to fail, as sketched at top centre.

Leonardo saw that the right side of the heart takes in blood from the venous system and that the left side pumps it into the arterial system, and he understood that this should empty the venous and fill the arterial system, but he never hinted at either pulmonary or systemic circulation. Instead, to keep the veins and arteries in balance, he concluded that some blood must pass back through the valves, despite his experiments that had shown perfect closure. This churning in and out of the blood was believed to provide the body's heat, which was regulated by the cooling air in the lungs, and the heat was thought to 'subtilise' the blood so that it acquired 'vital spirit', the life force that was distributed through the body by the arteries. Leonardo's work on the heart is thus a mix of acute observation – in some respects on a par with modern understanding – and ancient belief, and there is a mounting dissatis-faction in his notes as he tried to reconcile the two.

On moving to Rome in 1513, Leonardo tried to resume his anatomical studies at the hospital of Santo Spirito, but in a draft letter he complains of having been 'hindered in anatomy, denounced before the Pope and likewise at the hospital' by a troublesome German mirror-maker. Leonardo's anatomical career came to an undignified end, and he never completed his treatise. Though the existence of his anatomical studies was frequently mentioned by his early biographers, they were not properly understood until they were finally published in the years around 1900, and thus the work of one of the greatest of all anatomists had no discernible impact on the discipline.

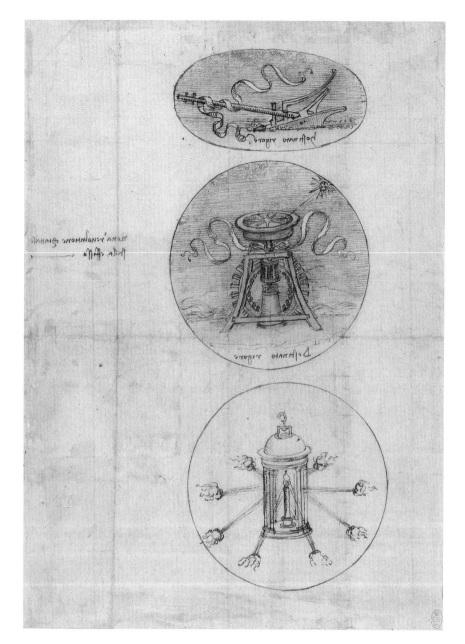

144

Three emblems, c.1508–10

Pen and ink, blue bodycolour, wash
of ground red chalk(?). 26.9 × 19.5 cm.
RCIN 912701

Each of these three emblems has the theme of constancy. At the top is a plough, with the motto *Hostinato rigore* ('Obstinate rigour'). At the centre is a compass mounted on a shaft, geared in a very Leonardesque manner to a waterwheel; the wheel is being turned by the water flowing below, but though this rotates the body of the compass, the needle points steadily at the sun. Beneath is the motto *Destinato rigore*, roughly 'determined rigour',

and in the margin, 'he is not turned around, who has such a fixed star'. Below, a candle at the centre of a lamp is blown by the eight winds and yet remains upright.

The sun in the second emblem contains three fleurs-de-lys, the symbol of the French king, and Leonardo was presumably designing these emblems for a courtier in occupied Milan who wished to express his steadfast devotion to Louis XII.

145
An allegory with a dog and an eagle, c.1508–10

Red chalk. 17.0 × 28.0 cm. RCIN 912496.
(See also pp. 184–5)

This is Leonardo's most highly finished chalk drawing, though its purpose is unknown, and the allegorical subject has received many different interpretations. The glorious eagle bestriding the earth wears a French crown with fleurs-de-lys, and must stand for the King of France; the animal in the boat is sometimes seen as a wolf representing the Pope, guiding the 'ship of the Church' (*navis ecclesiae*) with a tree for a mast. It has been seen as an allegory of the alliance between Pope Leo X and Francis I in 1515; of the marriage of Giuliano de' Medici (Leonardo's patron in Rome) and Philiberta of Savoy in 1516; of Ludovico Sforza fleeing to the protection of the Holy Roman Emperor in 1499; of Alexander VI cowering before the conquering Charles VIII in 1494; even as an allegory of canalisation projects in Lombardy.

The style of the landscape is that of the years around 1510 (cf. **98**), and the idea of a compass in turbulent waters remaining fixed on the glory of France is essentially the same as the central emblem of **144**. The animal in the boat is therefore presumably a dog, for fidelity, and the allegory expresses faithful devotion towards the King of France. Only the tree-mast is mysterious, though it could be a personal device of the patron.

146
A cloudburst of material possessions, c.1506–12

Black chalk, pen and ink. 11.7 × 11.1 cm.
Melzi's *184*. RCIN 912698

From thunderclouds a torrent of objects fall to earth – rakes, ladders, lanterns, bagpipes, shears, spectacles and so on – and written below is the lament 'Oh human misery, how many things you must serve for money.' But what might be a straightforward allegory of human materialism is complicated by a lion prowling in the clouds at top left, its head in two positions, and the note above, 'on this side Adam, on that, Eve'. If related to the drawing, the note might suggest the labours that mankind was subjected to after the Fall, contrasted with the unencumbered nobility of the lion, though that seems a rather strained reading.

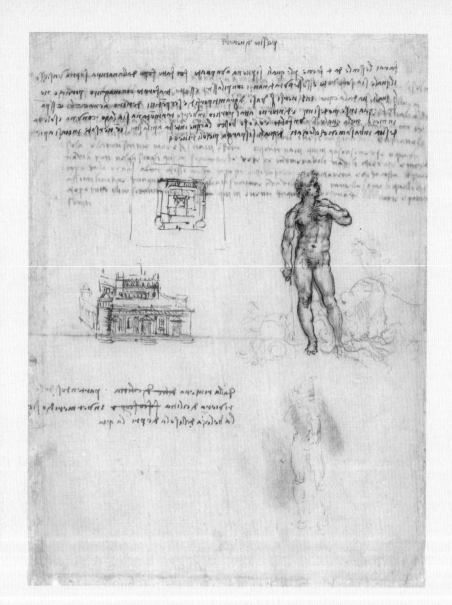

147
A palazzo, and a fountain of Neptune, c.1508–10

Black chalk, pen and ink.
27.0 × 20.1 CM. RCIN 912591

Leonardo was a member of the committee which met in January 1504 to decide where Michelangelo's newly completed sculpture of *David* (now Florence, Accademia) should be placed. Here he transforms Michelangelo's poised youth into a robust, middle-aged Neptune, with at least one sea-horse at his feet, in the manner of his drawing for Antonio Segni (**65**). The architectural studies are related to Leonardo's work after 1506 for the French occupiers of Milan, which included a projected suburban residence for the governor of the city, Charles d'Amboise. The square building drawn here features a combination of domestic and military motifs – a rich single-storey façade with niches and pedimented doors and windows, circular corner towers, and a square central tower with a deep courtyard.

The notes describe a pleasure garden inspired by the mythical gardens of Venus on Cyprus, featuring a natural meadow, a portico, fountains with vases of rare stones, a lake with an island, a shady wood and so on. This may have been envisaged for the grounds of Charles's residence, and it is possible that the *Neptune* was intended for a sculptural fountain in the gardens; but as so often, nothing came of these plans.

148
Designs for a water-clock, c.1508–10

Pen and ink. Two fragments, 8.4 × 5.9 cm
and 10.3 × 6.6 cm. RCIN S 912688, 912716

These fragments of a larger sheet (here reproduced in their original relationship) depict a water-clock, though the mechanism is obscure. The body of the clock is seen in plan at lower left, a cluster of 24 tubes of uniform height and increasing diameter, to be filled by a steady flow of water such that after one hour the first would be full, after two hours the second would also be full, and so on. At top right a figure is striking a large bell mounted over the device, though it is not apparent whether he is a living being who would simply observe how many tubes were full, or some sort of automaton. Two alternative and technically simpler designs at lower right consider dividing the body of the clock into 300 equal chambers (the sum of the numbers 1 to 24).

Leonardo had mentioned water-powered musical devices in his plans for the garden of Charles d'Amboise (**147**), an erudite reference to the amusements of antiquity described by Heron of Alexandria (see **153**), and it is quite possible that these designs were for the same project.

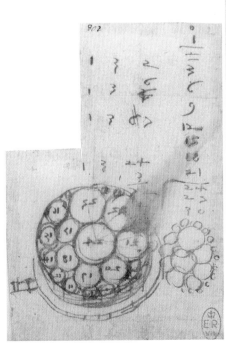
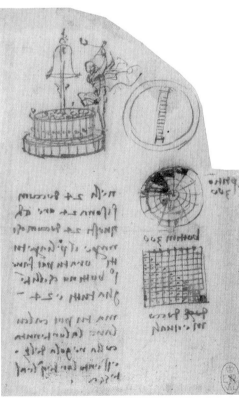

The Trivulzio monument

Almost two decades after the abortive project to cast a monument to Francesco Sforza (**40–48**), Leonardo had the opportunity to construct another equestrian monument, to Gian Giacomo Trivulzio (1440/41–1518), a *condottiere* or freelance military commander who had led the French in the invasion of Milan in 1499 and was appointed (briefly) governor of the city. Only one document is known for the monument, a detailed costing in Leonardo's own hand. From this we can infer that Trivulzio was to be represented in effigy on a sarcophagus supported by six harpies, on a marble platform with military trophies and captives (an echo of Michelangelo's tomb for Pope Julius II), and columns supporting an upper structure bearing an equestrian monument, as large as life. The equestrian group and the column capitals were to be bronze; the rest of the monument was to be marble, and Leonardo intended to subcontract the carving of those elements.

There is no evidence that Leonardo carried out any physical work on the monument. Instead a funerary chapel for Trivulzio was begun in 1512 to the designs of Bramantino, a tall square structure with an octagonal interior and the sarcophagi of Trivulzio and his family in high niches, attached like an atrium to the basilica of San Nazaro in Milan. Trivulzio's will of 1507 had made provision for a funerary chapel with a tomb monument in San Nazaro, but it is unclear how Leonardo's monument could have been integrated with Bramantino's chapel, and they probably belong to two phases of the project, with Leonardo's designs already abandoned when work started on the chapel.

Several drawings by Leonardo study the overall form of the monument (**149–151**) – unlike the Sforza monument, the base concerned him as much as the equestrian group. In **149**, Leonardo plays around with grandiose ideas for the base, a circular structure with an inner drum rising above a ring of columns (like Bramante's Tempietto in Rome, begun a few years earlier), a vast two-storeyed confection, or a four-sided classical structure containing a sarcophagus, with figures seated on the entablature. The fragment mounted at upper centre, cut from another sheet, shows the horse and rider placed directly on a sarcophagus, in the manner of a wall monument.

The sketch at lower left of **150** shows the monument as a three-arched structure, the central arch surmounted by an attic storey, but in the larger studies Leonardo's ambitions become more realistic and the sarcophagus sits within a relatively simple framework, either arched or square; captives are visible in the most heavily worked sketch, tethered to free-standing columns, with a detail at bottom left. In two studies the rearing horse is supported by a fallen foe, as in some of the earlier studies for the Sforza monument (**41**), and the study for the horse and rider alone shows Trivulzio apparently in contemporary armour.

149
Sketches for the Trivulzio monument, and other studies, c.1508–10

Pen and ink. 27.8 × 19.6 cm, with a fragment. 3.7 × 2.7 cm adhered. Melzi's *18* and *41*. RCIN 912353

150

Studies for the Trivulzio monument, c.1508–10

Pen and ink. 28.0 × 19.8 cm. Melzi's 17. RCIN 912355. (Detail shown pp. 18–19)

151 [OPPOSITE]

A study for the Trivulzio monument, c.1510–12

Red chalk, pen and ink. 21.7 × 16.9 cm. Melzi's 49. RCIN 912356

Leonardo seems to have been faced with the same issues of technical feasibility that he had encountered in the Sforza monument, and his later studies for the Trivulzio monument show the horse pacing rather than rearing. **151** contains many elements specified in the costing, with an effigy now seen on the sarcophagus. The horse rests his raised front hoof on a helmet, while the bare-headed Trivulzio raises his baton imperiously, rather than thrusting it forwards in the heat of battle. The penwork seems substantially later than in **149–150**, and it is not impossible that it was added some time after the red chalk; a tracing in black chalk and pen on the reverse of the sheet is distinctly late in style, and Leonardo may therefore have revisited his designs for the Trivulzio monument when he planned his final equestrian monument in France (**179–186**).

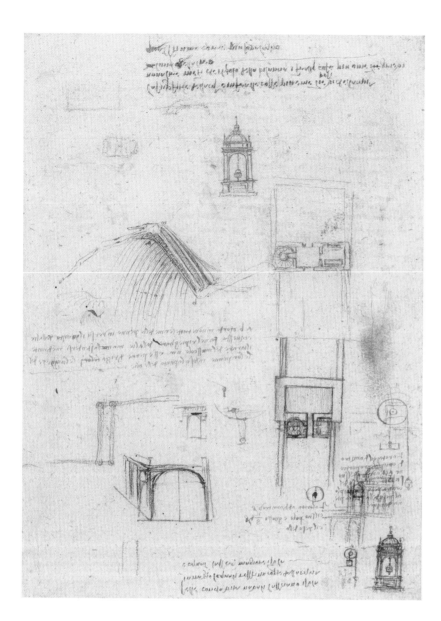

152

*Studies of architecture
and a bird's wing, c.1512–13*

Red chalk, pen and ink. 27.4 × 20.1 cm.
RCIN 919107v

During 1512 and 1513, after the expulsion of the French from Milan, Leonardo spent much time at the family villa of his pupil Francesco Melzi at Vaprio, 20 miles (30 km) to the north-east of the city (cf. **101**), and the architectural studies here are probably plans for improvements to the villa. At upper centre is an ornate wellhead, repeated at bottom right together with sketches of a simple winching mechanism, and the elevation of a façade obscured by the inscription; to centre right are two ground plans incorporating a spiral staircase. Further designs probably for the same project are seen on the reverse of **118**.

Leonardo continued to pursue his anatomical investigations while at Villa Melzi, working with oxen (**140–143**), dogs and birds (**137**). Here he studies the radius and ulna of a bird's wing, their joints arranged so that the humerus (to the right) and carpometacarpus (towards the wing tip) maintain approximately the same relative angle whatever the position of the wing. At lower left Leonardo reduces this to a simple system of rods hinged in a long parallelogram, no doubt thinking how to reproduce the mechanics of a bird's wing in his projected flying machine.

153
Designs for fountains,
c.1513

Red chalk, pen and ink,
on blue paper. Two fragments,
15.0 × 6.0 cm and 17.2 × 6.3 cm.
RCINS 912690, 912691

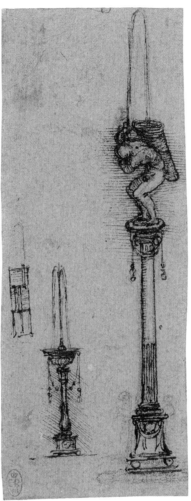

On two fragments probably cut from a single sheet are designs for a 'Heron's fountain', a hydraulic curiosity invented by Heron (or Hero) of Alexandria in the first century AD. Leonardo shows the arrangement of the reservoirs and tubes schematically in a small cross-section: water flows by gravity through a tube from an upper reservoir into a sealed lower chamber, displacing air upwards through another tube into a central reservoir almost filled with water; the air pressure forces the water in the central reservoir upwards through a third tube, to create a fountain playing into the upper

reservoir. The device gives the impression of being a perpetual motion machine, though eventually the upper reservoir empties and the fountain stops.

The designs offer a rare glimpse of Leonardo thinking as a sculptor in a context other than an equestrian monument. Their scale is hard to determine: they were probably table fountains to be cast in bronze or silver, but the columns seem monumental in conception and they could have been full-scale fountains for a garden (cf. **147**). The distinctive technique dates the drawings to the end of Leonardo's time in Milan.

The Madonna and Child with St Anne

The subject of the *Madonna and Child with St Anne*, with either a lamb or the infant Baptist, occupied Leonardo intermittently for the last two decades of his life. The original commission possibly came from the French king Louis XII (whose consort was Anne of Brittany) soon after the invasion of Milan in 1499. Leonardo was working on the composition after returning to Florence in 1500, eventually producing three distinct full-size compositions, of which a cartoon (fig. 18) and a painting (fig. 19) survive in the original.

When Fra Pietro da Novellara visited Leonardo's workshop in Florence in April 1501 (see **64**), he saw an unfinished 'sketch on a large sheet of paper [*cartone*]', depicting the Christ Child slipping out of his mother's arms to embrace a lamb (signifying the Passion).[22] The Madonna was taking hold of the Child to separate him from the lamb, while St Anne restrained her daughter from this; the figures were life-sized and all seated or bent over, one in front of another to the left. The cartoon is lost but known through painted variants.

It was probably that cartoon that was displayed in Leonardo's workshop at Santissima Annunziata, according to Giorgio Vasari writing half a century later (though Vasari described both the infant Baptist and a lamb, conflating Leonardo's treatments of the subject): 'Men and women, young and old, continued for two days to flock for a sight of it […] as if to a solemn festival, in order to gaze at the marvels of Leonardo.'[23] Vasari also stated that when Leonardo later travelled to France, it was to 'colour the cartoon of St Anne', and, as we shall see, this is partly true.[24]

In October 1503, the Florentine humanist Agostino Vespucci annotated a passage in an edition of Cicero's letters, in which the Roman statesman described the technique of the Greek painter Apelles, perfecting the head of a Venus but leaving the body roughly finished. Vespucci noted 'so Leonardo da Vinci does in all his pictures [*in omnibus suis picturis*], such as the head of Lisa del Giocondo [the *Mona Lisa*], and Anne, Mother of the Virgin'.[25] It has been supposed that Vespucci was referring to the Louvre painting, and that this was therefore substantially complete by 1503. But the evidence of the preparatory drawings makes such an early date for the painting impossible, and Vespucci was surely

referring to the first cartoon, evidently well known in Florence. (Nor does Vespucci's comment demonstrate that the *Mona Lisa* was complete by late 1503, only that a significant start had been made on the painting.)

For whatever reason, Leonardo then executed a second cartoon of the subject (fig. 18), featuring the infant Baptist instead of a lamb, whose composition was developed almost in its entirety in a single densely worked study in the British Museum. The style of both the drawing and the cartoon point to a date around 1506–8. But again, Leonardo (or his patron) must have been dissatisfied, and from about 1508 onwards he developed a third composition, reverting to the lamb. This was executed as a painting (fig. 19), which was recorded in Leonardo's studio in France in October 1517, and remained unfinished in the foreground landscape and the lower drapery of St Anne.

A dozen studies of details for the Louvre panel are known, of a range of dates. It was not Leonardo's working method to finalise all the details in a preparatory cartoon, which then simply had to be rendered in paint. The London cartoon is more of a full-scale sketch, with the faces and drapery carefully drawn but many details improvised or indistinct. If a similar cartoon had been produced for the Louvre painting, or if Leonardo had worked out the composition directly on the panel, he would have had to make studies to clarify details as he worked on the painting – and that is exactly what the drawings suggest. The order of the drawings correlates with the level of execution of the corresponding part of the painting: the earlier drawings are for portions entirely executed by Leonardo; the later are for portions where the hand of an assistant is more evident, or (as in **159**) not finished.

The drawing in **154** has commonly been associated with the *St Anne* project, though it does not correspond closely with the Christ Child or Baptist in any of the versions. The style is that of the Leda studies (fig. 13) or, in the charcoal, the *Neptune* (**65**), and this may be a sheet of 'background studies' towards the second cartoon, made when the iconography shifted from a lamb to the infant Baptist. Leonardo's aim would have been to capture lifelike and spontaneous poses and gestures, with no regard as to how they might be integrated in a multi-figure composition.

FIG.18
The Madonna and Child with St Anne and the Infant Baptist,
*c.*1506–8. Charcoal, wash, white chalk, on paper mounted
on canvas. 141.5 × 104.6 cm. London, National Gallery

FIG.19
*The Madonna and Child with St Anne and a lamb, c.*1508–19.
Oil on panel. 168.4 × 113 cm. Paris, Louvre

Two sketches for a composition with the lamb, in Paris and Venice, are difficult to date – it is not even certain which version they are for. The earliest studies reliably for the painting are three red-on-red drawings for Christ, which indicate that its execution was under way by around 1508–10 when Leonardo was back in Milan working for the French, and perhaps trying to fulfil a commission for Louis XII that was already ten years overdue.

The other preparatory drawings for the painting date from the last decade of Leonardo's life, though the development of his pictorial style during this period – especially his years in Rome from 1513 to 1516 – is poorly understood. The study for the head of St Anne, **155**, corresponds in pose with the head in the painting, though as in most of his studies of women the conventional downwards gaze occupied Leonardo little (cf. **67**–**68**). Instead he lavished his attention on a folded and twisted headdress that dwarfs the facial features of the saint, which in the painting were enlarged and regularised. The soft handling of the black chalk is comparable to a number of landscape studies that may also be associated with the painting (**103**).

The drawing **156** is one of the most puzzling of Leonardo's sheets. It is often connected with the *St Anne* compositions, and the pose is that of St Anne in the first cartoon (as known through copies); but the headdress

154
Studies of an infant, c.1504–8

Charcoal, pen and ink. 20.5 × 15.2 cm. Melzi's *202*. RCIN 912562

is similar to that of St Anne in the painting, and the technique dates the drawing no earlier than 1510. The face is that of a young woman, and it seems rather indistinctly modelled for Leonardo – it was possibly worked up by a later hand, for damage to the sheet from having been framed suggests that it had a different route into the Royal Collection from the other Leonardo drawings. The lack of a direct correspondence with any of the versions of the *St Anne* may suggest instead that it is a study for an unrelated Madonna – there is documentary evidence of several late paintings by Leonardo of the *Madonna and Child*, of which we have no trace.

155
The head of St Anne, c.1510–15

Black chalk. 18.8 × 13.0 cm. RCIN 912533

156 [PAGE 197]
The head of the Madonna(?), c.1510–15

Red and black chalks, brush and ink, white heightening, on orange-red prepared paper. 24.4 × 18.7 cm. RCIN 912534

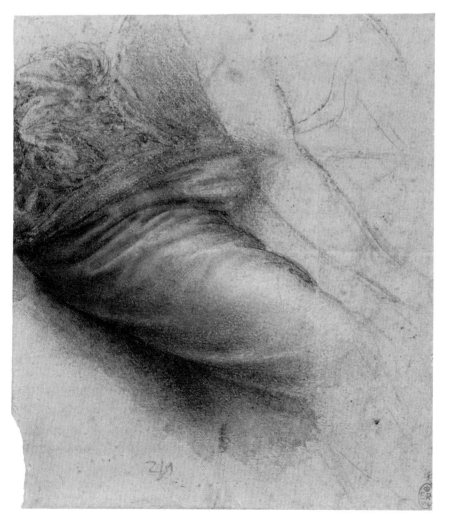

157
The drapery of the Madonna's arm, c.1510–15

Red and black chalks, wash, white heightening, pen and ink, on orange-red prepared paper. 8.6 × 17.0 cm. Melzi's *213*. RCIN 912532

158
The drapery of the Madonna's thigh, c.1515–17

Charcoal, black chalk partly washed over, touches of brown wash, white heightening. 16.4 × 14.5 cm. Melzi's *219*. RCIN 912530. (Detail shown p. 1)

159
The drapery of St Anne's legs,
c.1517–18

Black and white chalks on paper
washed buff. 16.7 × 14.7 cm.
Melzi's *226*. RCIN 912527

Leonardo's most impressive drawings for the *St Anne* are the drapery studies. **157** is for the right arm of the Virgin, a swirl of concertina folds swelling at the elbow, a device that he had used earlier in the angel of the *Virgin of the Rocks* (fig. 7) and St Peter in the *Last Supper* (**61**). The technique combines chalk, wash, heightening and a ground all of different colours, capturing not just the form of the sleeve but also the effect of layered glazes in the painting, and allowing such drawings to serve as a guide for assistants working on the painting.

The technique is just as rich in **158**, with a combination of charcoal and black chalk partly washed over to blend the modelling, and white heightening applied with the delicacy and precision of a miniaturist; but the colouristic range is now compressed due to Leonardo's late abandonment of red chalk. And **159**, for the drapery of St Anne's legs, is drawn with a combination of smooth blended strokes and accents with a finely sharpened chalk, on French paper prepared with a buff wash; a second study of the same drapery (RCIN 912526) is on paper with a dark grey preparation, a characteristic of some of Leonardo's final sheets (cf. **199**).

These are the last of Leonardo's drawings towards a painting, and demonstrate that he never lost his desire to explore the graphic possibilities of his limited range of media, in the search for the most sophisticated effects of light in his paintings.

Ideal male heads

Leonardo established his two standard male types early in his career (4), an adolescent with straight nose, lightly rounded chin and open expression, and an older man with aquiline nose, prominent chin and beetling brow. They became noticeably more classical when he moved in the 1480s to Milan, where such heads in profile – inspired by ancient coins and medals – were a common decorative motif adorning all manner of objects, from buildings to the borders of manuscripts. From Leonardo's return to Milan in 1506 until the end of his life he produced a number of independent drawings of heads, exercises in form and draughtsmanship simply for his own satisfaction.

In **160** the use of red chalk on red prepared paper limits the tonal contrasts in the face to give the smoothly rounded surface of a layer of juvenile fat, while the black chalk of the hair mingles with the red in a dense pattern of corkscrew curls. **161**, by contrast, is drawn in the refined black chalk style of Leonardo's latest sheets; like many of Leonardo's bust-length studies, the shoulders (clad in a low-cut gathered chemise) are turned in three-quarters view while the head remains in strict profile. The curly hair of these two drawings was a feature of Roman busts of the Hadrianic period, but Leonardo's fascination with such hair may have had a more personal origin. In 1490 the ten-year-old Gian Giacomo Caprotti, known as Salaì, entered Leonardo's studio as an assistant, staying with him until the artist's death 29 years later. Gian Paolo Lomazzo wrote in 1584 of the homosexual nature of the relationship between Leonardo and Salaì, and in 1568 Giorgio Vasari described Salaì as 'a very attractive youth of unusual grace and looks, with beautiful hair which he wore curled in ringlets and which delighted his master'.[26] While Leonardo's youthful profiles are not portraits of Salaì, it is plausible that his ideal of male beauty was transformed by his relationship with the maturing boy.

160 [OPPOSITE]

The head of a youth, c.1510

Red and black chalks on orange-red prepared paper. 21.7 × 15.3 cm. Melzi's 34.
RCIN 912554

161

The head of a youth, c.1517–18

Black chalk. 19.3 × 14.9 cm. Melzi's 26.
RCIN 912557

162

The head of a bearded man, c.1517–18

Black chalk. 17.8 × 13.0 cm.
Melzi's 40. RCIN 912553

163 [OPPOSITE]

The bust of a man, c.1510

Red and black chalks on orange-red
prepared paper. 22.2 × 15.9 cm.
RCIN 912556

Leonardo's young men were always images of beauty,
but the older type was more varied. In Florence he was
rather rustic, and around 1490 Leonardo distorted him
to produce entertaining grotesques (**49, 52**). But as
Leonardo himself aged, so his older men were presented
with greater sympathy and gravitas. **162** is a virile man
with thick-set neck and determined brow, hair like the
waves in the most stylised *Deluges* (**197**), and a beard that
may be a reflection of the fashion at the court of Francis I.

The finest example of the middle-aged 'warrior' type
is **163**, a counterpart of **161** in its combination of chalks,
but with the smoothness of that drawing replaced by
wide variations of surface texture that convey a sense of
slack skin over firm muscle – areas of chalk rubbed into
the surface, stumping, wetting the tip of the chalk, and
accents in black chalk around the facial features as well
as the hair.

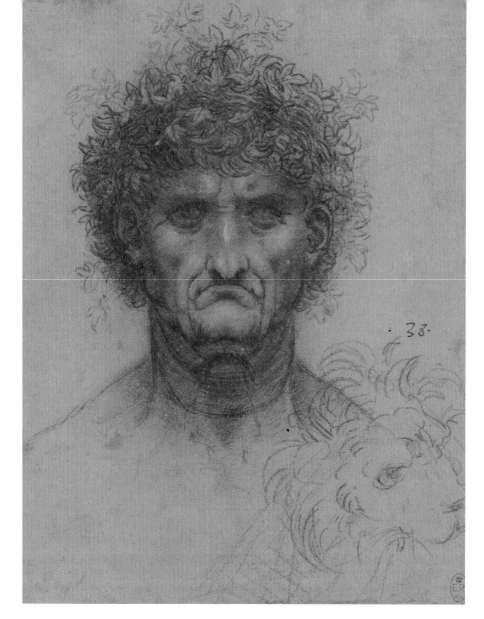

164
The bust of a man, c.1510

Red chalk, touches of white chalk,
on orange-red prepared paper.
18.3 × 13.6 cm. Melzi's 38. RCIN 912502

165 [OPPOSITE]
*The head of an old
bearded man, c.1517–18*

Black chalk. 21.3 × 15.5 cm.
Melzi's 29. RCIN 912499

In **164** Leonardo turns the same head to the front, with a hint of the grotesque as the nose almost meets the clamped mouth, and a wreath of ivy leaves and a lion skin across the shoulder that identify him as a 'wild man'. Leonardo had designed costumes of wild men for festivities in 1491, though this drawing dates from two decades later; the wild man was an emblem of Gian Giacomo Trivulzio, Leonardo's patron around 1510 (**149–151**), and it is just possible that the drawing was made in connection with some project for Trivulzio.

The profile of **165** is that of Leonardo's usual toothless old man, but he is far from pitiful: the neck is vigorously muscular, the beard luxuriant, and the long hair twisted into plaits suggesting a certain exoticism, as if he were an oriental magus. Just as the youthful profile may in some subliminal way be a 'portrait' of Salaì, so Leonardo may have come to regard its pendant, the older man, as at some level a self-image (and that seems abundantly true of **200**). A copy of the drawing executed by Lucas Vorsterman in the 1620s (British Museum), soon after the original arrived in England, is inscribed as a portrait of Leonardo, reflecting the common conception of Leonardo in later centuries as a mystical seer.

166

Assistant of Leonardo

A sketch of Leonardo, the head of a youth, and a horse's legs, c.1517–18

Pen and ink, black chalk. 26.0 × 16.7 cm.
Melzi's 23. RCIN 912300v

Both sides of the sheet contain studies by Leonardo of a horse's leg, for his late equestrian monument (cf. **183**). The sheet was then used by an assistant to sketch two heads, a handsome smiling youth and a pensive old man with a full beard (and Francesco Melzi's placing of his number 23 indicates that he considered that to be the most important study on the sheet). Comparison with the formal portrait of Leonardo by Melzi (**1**), which must be close in date, strongly suggests that this too is a depiction of Leonardo: the long straight nose, the line of the beard rising diagonally up the cheek to the ear, a ringlet falling from the moustache at the corner of the mouth, and the long hair falling from the back of the head are all exactly as in **1**.

Other than Melzi's portrait, this is the only contemporary likeness of Leonardo, here aged about 65. He seems perhaps a little world-weary, but the presence of the sketch alongside studies for yet another grand equestrian monument shows that his ambitions were undimmed.

167

Attributed to Francesco Melzi (1491/3–c.1570)

The castle of Amboise, c.1516–19

Red chalk. 13.3 × 26.3 cm. Melzi's *173*. RCIN 912727

Leonardo travelled from Rome to the Loire valley in central France in late 1516, and was given apartments in the manor house of Clos Lucé, half a mile to the south of the castle at Amboise. This drawing depicts the castle as seen from Leonardo's residence (the opposite side from the usual views of the castle, from the river). The drawing may even have been made from the windows of Leonardo's apartments, but it is not by Leonardo himself, and his assistant and eventual heir Francesco Melzi is perhaps the likeliest candidate.

From ancient foundations the castle had grown haphazardly, and though Charles VIII had imported Italian designers during the 1490s to remodel the castle, when Leonardo arrived it was still a jumble of buildings of different periods within a rambling curtain wall, essentially medieval in plan. The view shows the principal buildings to the left of centre, a large low circular tower in the defensive walls below, a gate and wooden bridge over a ravine to the right, and a cluster of cottages below the walls at left.

168
A design for a palace,
c.1517–18

Black chalk. 18.0 × 24.5 cm. Melzi's *20* (recto). RCIN 912292v

The drawing is sketched on the reverse of a study of a horse's leg, for Leonardo's late equestrian monument (cf. **166**, **179–186**). It depicts a vast rectangular palace of three storeys, with square towers or pavilions at each corner and in the middle of each side. Bridges to either side of the palace, terracing down from the long flank, and a foreground that slopes and tapers towards us, all seem to indicate the palace was intended for a long, narrow river island. This topography corresponds with that of the island at Amboise (the Île St-Jean or Île d'Or), which to this day is reached from either bank by twin bridges at the south-western end of the island.

Around the same time Leonardo drew a simplified map of the island, with bridges at the same points, to study the currents in the Loire (Codex Arundel, fol. 269r). There is no indication of a projected palace on that map, and the focus of Leonardo's architectural activity in France was at Romorantin, 30 miles (50 km) to the east. But so well does the topography of this sketch correspond with Amboise that Leonardo must have envisaged a grand new palace on the island, to supersede the jumble of buildings – some of them very recent – of the castle at Amboise, as seen in **167**.

169
A woman in a landscape,
c.1517–18

Black chalk. 21.0 × 13.5 cm. Melzi's *216*. RCIN 912581

The most plausible explanation of this mysterious drawing is that it depicts Matelda, appearing to Dante in *Purgatory* (Cantos 28–29), the second book of his *Divine Comedy*: 'I came upon a stream that blocked / the path of my advance; [...] / I halted, and I set my eyes upon / the farther bank, to look at the abundant / variety of newly-flowered boughs; / And there [...] / I saw a solitary woman moving, / singing, and gathering up flower on flower. / [...] No sooner had she reached the point where that / fair river's waves could barely bathe the grass, / than she gave me this gift: lifting her eyes. / [...] / Erect, along the farther bank, she smiled, / her hands entwining varicoloured flowers.'

The fluttering drapery here echoes that of Matelda in Botticelli's illustration of the same scene (Berlin, Kupferstichkabinett), though the distinctive pose is derived from a figure in one of Mantegna's canvases of the *Triumph of Caesar*, the *Bearers of Trophies and Bullion* (*c*.1484–92; Royal Collection, RCIN 403960), perhaps known to Leonardo via a print. The pointing gesture and direct gaze relate the drawing to Leonardo's compositions of the *Angel of the Annunciation* (see **73**) and *St John the Baptist* (Paris, Louvre), and would put us here in the position of Dante, as Matelda indicates her earthly paradise to us. But Leonardo had, it seems, little sustained interest in Dante, and most quotations from the *Divine Comedy* in his notebooks are on natural phenomena; though the background here is hard to read it seems rocky, and we know from the *Leda* that Leonardo would not miss an opportunity to illustrate a flowery setting (see **105–110**). The context and function of the drawing thus remain unknown.

Costume studies

Only from the end of Leonardo's life do we have a significant number of detailed costume drawings, **170–176**, which give some idea of the rich dress that he must have devised on several occasions during his career, for festivals, theatrical performances and so on. Francis I had a taste for lavish entertainments, and in letters sent from the French court to Mantua we find detailed descriptions of festivities held in 1518 – in honour of the young Federico Gonzaga, then completing his education at the French court, and to celebrate the baptism of the Dauphin and the wedding of the King's niece Madeleine de la Tour d'Auvergne to Lorenzo di Piero de' Medici (for whom Leonardo had briefly worked three years earlier in Florence). For instance at one event Federico Gonzaga was described as:

> very showy, dressed as a lansquenet, with half-boots, one completely dark, the other less dark, edged with a white and yellow riband cut in the German manner, a tunic half of satin, the edge of silver cloth, and golden cloth made into scales, with a German-style shirt worked with gold, and over this a cape of dark cloth fitted with a riband of gold and silver cloth made in the French manner.[27]

The richness and layering of textiles described in the letters is exactly what Leonardo was aiming at in **170–174**, with ribbons, plumes, fringes, spotted furs, and quilted sleeves and breeches. But the use of parti-coloured material carried a loaded meaning – striped, checked and scalloped clothing was associated with mercenary soldiers (as in the lansquenet of **170**), fools, minstrels and prostitutes; the dignified guests of Francis I were dressing up not just exotically, but in something risqué. The atmospheric handling of the black chalk in **172–174** is that of Leonardo's last years, and the drawings are close enough in their effect of multi-layered elegance, and in many details, to suggest that they are studies for costumes to be worn at such events, and that one of Leonardo's roles at the French court was to provide designs for the King's seamstresses.

170 [OPPOSITE]

A masquerader as a lansquenet, c.1517–18

Black chalk, pen and ink, wash, on rough paper.
27.3 × 18.3 cm. Melzi's 86. RCIN 912575

171

A masquerader on horseback, c.1517–18

Black chalk, pen and ink, on rough paper.
24.0 × 15.2 cm. Melzi's 87. RCIN 912574

The figures in **172–173** appear rather androgynous, but their stance, with clearly visible legs planted well apart, rules out the possibility that they were intended to be women. The youth in **172** holds the edge of a long skirt up to his waist, showing the scalloped edges of his tunic and a sheer underskirt, while in **173** he wears an even more ornate tunic and a full sheer skirt that displays the whole of both legs. The figure in **174**, by contrast, has a high-waisted dress and pronounced bust, and must be female. The hairstyle, however,

appears to be the same as in **173**, wound around the head and knotted, with a tail emerging from the knot, and groomed at the front into a shell-like crest – the convergence of male and female to a single ideal type, with smooth, fleshy features, is a marked aspect of Leonardo's late work. The red chalk is indistinct but coincides too closely with the forms of the figure to be accidental offsetting, and must have been lightly rubbed on by Leonardo to give colouristic effect unusual in his late drawings.

172 [OPPOSITE, LEFT]

A standing masquerader,
c.1517–18

Black chalk. 21.4 × 10.7 cm.
Melzi's 85. RCIN 912577

173 [OPPOSITE, RIGHT]

A standing masquerader,
c.1517–18

Black chalk. 21.5 × 11.2 cm.
Melzi's 84. RCIN 912576

174

The bust of a masquerader
in right profile, c.1517–18

Black chalk, rubbed with red chalk.
17.0 × 14.6 cm. Melzi's 39.
RCIN 912508

A quite different type of costume is seen in **175** – a prisoner with picturesquely tattered clothes, his ankles shackled, ropes tied from the shackle to his waist (forcing his knees to bend) and his neck, leaning on a rustic club and begging for alms. As with the other costume studies, the paper is French, and this was probably a costume to be worn at the same or a similar festivity, to heighten the effect of the luxuriously dressed protagonists of **170–174**.

The image in **176** also appears to be a study for a costume, to house two men in the manner of a panto-mime horse. A clawed arm sketched in black chalk can be seen emerging from the side of the head, at the natural height of a man whose legs form the front legs of the beast and who supports the oversized head on his shoulders as in a Chinese festival dragon. The paper is Italian but the style of the drawing is very late, and it may tentatively be associated with the festivities at the French court.

175
A costume study of a prisoner,
c.1517–18

Black chalk. 18.4 × 12.7 cm. Inscribed *ojo*.
RCIN 912573

176
A design for a dragon costume,
c.1517–18

Black chalk, pen and ink. 18.8 × 27.0 cm.
Melzi's 29. RCIN 912369

177

Cats, lions and a dragon, c.1517–18

Black chalk, pen and ink, wash.
27.0 × 21.0 cm. RCIN 912363

These two sheets are close in style, though the rougher paper of **178** has caused the ink to bleed. More than 40 separate studies cover the full range of Leonardo's modes, from the most acutely observed and unaffected in his studies of domestic cats, to the most stylised and 'Leonardesque' in the coiling dragons. The studies on **177** of sleeping cats must have been done directly from the life, whereas the cats fighting had to be visualised on the basis of fleeting impressions (cf. **115–117**). In eight further drawings across the two sheets Leonardo shows a good understanding of the proportions of a lioness, which he would have known from the lions kept caged behind the Palazzo della Signoria in Florence as symbols of the city.

On **178** Leonardo depicted the horses in a variety of extreme attitudes, and five vignettes of St George fighting a dragon serve the same purpose, giving a context to the twisting of the horse away from the monster. The notes on both sheets show that Leonardo's concern was the range of movements attainable by animals: 'Of flexion and extension. The lion is prince of this animal species because of the flexibility of its spine'; and 'Serpentine movement is the principal action in animals, and is double, the first along its length and the second across its width.' In a notebook of c.1513–14 Leonardo proposed 'a treatise on the movements of animals with four feet, among which is man, who in his infancy crawls on all fours'.[28] That was perhaps displacement activity for Leonardo's stalled work on human anatomy, and there is no sustained evidence, beyond these drawings of a few years later, that he developed a treatise on animal motion in any detail.

178

Horses, St George fighting the dragon, and a lion, c.1517–18

Black chalk, pen and ink, wash, on rough paper.
29.8 × 21.2 cm. Melzi's *115* (and *46* crossed out). RCIN 912331

A late equestrian monument

Late in life Leonardo planned a third equestrian monument, following on from the abandoned monument to Francesco Sforza (**40–48**) and the unexecuted Trivulzio monument (**149–151**). The only evidence of this putative late project is a coherent group of drawings studying a rearing or pacing horse (with or without a rider) and the anatomy of the horse. All are drawn on French paper in Leonardo's delicate late style, in black chalk occasionally reinforced with pen and ink.

In most studies the rider is shown in antique robes, and where he is in modern armour (RCIN 912343) he is not recognisable as a portrait. One study on **179** includes the props of a tortoise and a pouring ewer, symbols of constancy and bounty, the qualities of a beneficent ruler rather than a military leader, and it is quite possible that Leonardo's employer, the young Francis I, was the intended subject. But Leonardo seems not to have attempted large-scale or physically demanding work in his last years, and he did not put his mind to the practicalities of modelling or casting the sculpture.

In the two central studies of **179** Leonardo returns to his first ambitions for both the Sforza and Trivulzio monuments, with the horse rearing over a fallen foe, but the designs are more compact than in **41** or **150**, almost circular in outline and reminiscent of a coin or medal. In the larger study the raised foot of the fallen soldier supports the chest of the horse, so that its front legs are free, while the rider, in a fluttering cloak, raises a spear to strike. In the smaller study to the left, the rider, crowned with laurels, gazes resolutely forwards with no regard for the foe (perhaps a dragon) beneath his horse. The other studies show the horse in a walking pose, the rider brandishing a baton forwards or backwards. In two of the drawings a pedestal is outlined, a low rectangular structure with simple pilasters at the corners, and in the more finished study indications of a basin to receive the water flowing from the ewer.

179
Designs for an equestrian monument, c.1517–18

Black chalk, pen and ink. 22.4 × 16.0 cm.
Melzi's *121*. RCIN 912360. (Detail shown right)

180

Designs for an equestrian monument, c.1517–18

Black chalk. 26.7 × 16.1 cm. Melzi's *12*.
RCIN 912359

181 [OPPOSITE]

Designs for an equestrian monument, c.1517–18

Black chalk. 27.8 × 18.4 cm. Melzi's *19*.
RCIN 912342

The upper horse of **180** has a pacing gait, with both legs on the same side advanced, an unnatural movement for which horses must be trained. This is the pose of Donatello's *Gattamelata* and Verrocchio's *Colleoni*, and would have indicated to a contemporary, much more aware of horsemanship than we are, the qualities of culture and control. But in a sculpture this pose requires the advanced rear leg to be grounded or supported, to stabilise the monument; Leonardo usually preferred the natural walk, with diagonally-opposed legs grounded (as in central study) to balance the monument. The lower study is one of Leonardo's most ingenious solutions to the problem of stability – as the rider reins in the horse, which seems to recoil from a dog yapping beneath its raised front hoof, most of the weight is taken on the rear legs.

The two principal studies of **181** show the horse walking, its head held in a variety of positions – the shimmering outline of the upper study is remarkable even among Leonardo's late drawings. The rider is again crowned with laurels: in the upper study he holds the baton in his lap, while below he thrusts it forwards while turning his body backwards. Four small, faint studies to left and below examine further permutations of horse and rider.

182

Designs for an equestrian monument, c.1517–18

Black chalk, pen and ink. 20.3 × 14.3 cm.
Melzi's 89. RCIN 912344

The upper study of **182** shows the horse in strict profile, but below are two oblique views from behind with the neck twisted in opposite directions, examining the effect of turning the horse's head towards or away from the raised foreleg. The rectangular outline of the pedestal demonstrates that Leonardo had the requirements of a sculpture in his mind, and was not simply playing a game of variations on the outline of the horse.

Along with the studies of the whole monument, Leonardo made a series of detailed studies of the anatomy of the horse, in the walking pose planned for the sculpture. Though he knew the form of the horse intimately, he felt the need to study it afresh, as he had for the early *Adorations* (**6–10**), the Sforza monument, and the *Battle of Anghiari* (**71–83**). Some of these are formally laid out, such as **183**, studying the chest and forelegs with the right leg raised, and the rear of the horse; comparison with the same aspect in **45** reveals how Leonardo's equine ideal had evolved since the Sforza horse, for the animal here is much more heavily built.

Other drawings in the series may appear casually done from the life, such as **184** of a raised left hind leg from four viewpoints, but this is exactly the intended pose of the sculpture. The main study is supremely elegant, the smooth contours hatched and cross-hatched with curving lines that follow the form of the body. The cruder pen drawing at upper left corresponds exactly with a retouched study for one of the early *Adorations* (RCIN 912311), in which the metalpoint was drawn almost 40 years earlier but the outlines were redrawn in pen in this same late style, demonstrating that to the end of his life Leonardo continued to refer to his earliest drawings.

183 [OPPOSITE]

Studies of a horse, c.1517–18

Black chalk, pen and ink, on paper
washed buff. 23.3 × 16.5 cm. RCIN 912303

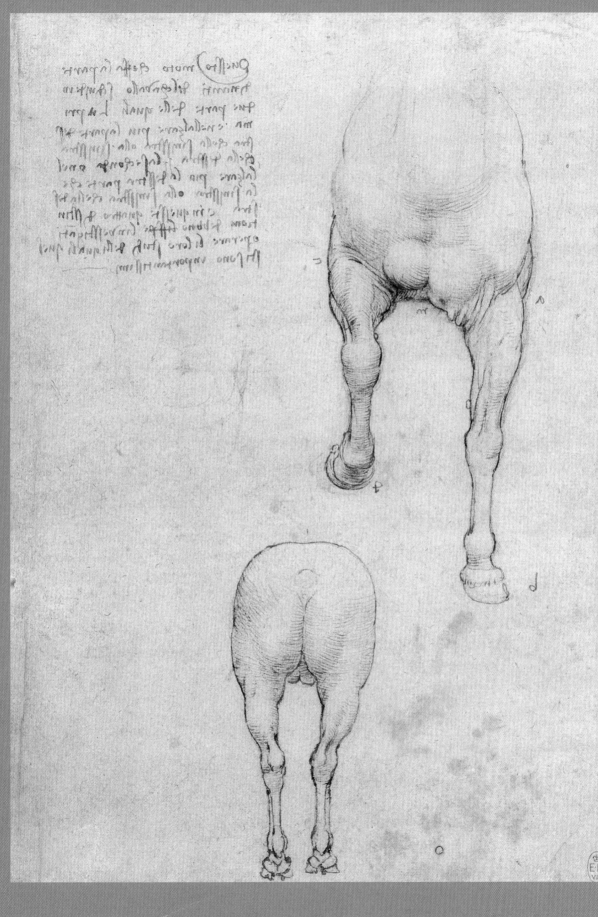

184

Studies of a horse, c.1517–18

Black chalk, pen and ink, on paper washed buff.
20.3 × 15.8 cm. Melzi's *119*. RCIN 912313

185

A study of a horse, c.1517–18

Black chalk. 25.0 × 17.4 cm. Melzi's *15*.
RCIN 912309V

On the reverse of another study of the horse's legs is
185, a glimpse in black chalk of the muscular horse from
three-quarters behind, in foreshortening and a little
from below, as if looking up at the monument on its
pedestal. Though this is one of the most sketchily drawn
studies it is also one of the most evocative, conveying
the weight and majesty of Leonardo's conception.

What may be Leonardo's final study for an equestrian
monument is to be found on **186**. The drawing stands
apart from the other late equestrian studies: the horse
is even more barrel-chested, the rider rather rubbery
and doll-like, and nude apart from a cascading cloak.
He raises his arm to strike his fallen foe, who as in **179**
pushes his foot up into the chest of the horse. The
lightly sketched pedestal features a deep cornice, the
frieze with a trophy at the centre, standing on two piers
each with pilasters at the corners. The uncertain sense
of scale and hazy black chalk give the drawing a dream-
like atmosphere. This is no longer a practical study: it is
Leonardo's last, grandest expression of a concept that
he had worked on for many years, and that he now
knew would only ever be realised on paper.

186 [OPPOSITE]

*A design for an equestrian
monument, c.1518–19*

Black chalk on paper washed buff.
20.1 × 12.4 cm. Melzi's *45*. RCIN 912354

Deluges

A cataclysmic storm overwhelming the earth was one of Leonardo's favourite subjects during the last years of his life, in both his drawings and his writings. Several long passages recount the futile struggles of man and animal against the overwhelming forces of nature – tempests, floods, a mountain collapsing on a city, and finally the storm sweeping away all matter. It is surely not fanciful to see this obsession with death and destruction as the deeply personal expression of an artist nearing his end – an artist who had seen some of his greatest creations unfinished or destroyed before his eyes, and who had a profound sense of the impermanence of all things, even of the earth itself.

But Leonardo's descriptions of the deluge, far from being chaotic, are objective and detached, emphasising the attitudes of the figures, the appearance of the land-scape, the optical qualities of cloud, rain, water, debris, dust and smoke, and thus of a piece with his notes throughout his life towards a treatise on painting, with every effect of interest to the painter now amplified and thrown together. As always, Leonardo was attempting to analyse as many specific cases as possible, and some-times his writings digress bathetically into simple dynamics.

One of these long passages can be seen in **187**, running to almost 1,000 words on each side of the sheet, and laid out like a scientific treatise with marginal illustrations – a coastal view with rainfall, a plan of a dam with water flooding through a breach, a cloud formation with a downpour, a whirlpool sucking boats to its centre, a wave striking a block and curling back on itself, a wave breaking, and water flowing down a sluice. Not all the text can be quoted here, but a couple of passages give the flavour:

Description of the deluge:

Let there first be shown the summit of a rugged mountain surrounded by valleys. From its sides the soil slides together with the roots of bushes, denuding great areas of rock. And descending from these precipices, ruinous in its boisterous course, it lays bare the twisted and gnarled roots of large trees, throwing their roots upwards; and the mountains, scoured bare, reveal deep fissures made by ancient earthquakes. The bases of the mountains are covered with ruins of trees hurled down from their lofty peaks, mixed with mud, roots, branches and leaves thrust into the mud and earth and stones.

And into the depths of a valley the fragments of a mountain have fallen, forming a shore to the swollen waters of its river, which has burst its banks and rushes on in monstrous waves, striking and destroying the walls of the towns and farmhouses in the valley. The ruin of these buildings throws up a great dust, rising like smoke or wreathed clouds against the falling rain. The swollen waters sweep round them, striking these obstacles in eddying whirlpools, and leaping into the air as muddy foam. And the whirling waves fly from the place of concussion, and their impetus moves them across other eddies in a contrary direction [...]

The rain as it falls from the clouds is of the same colour as those clouds, in its shaded side, unless the sun's rays break through them, in which case the rain will appear less dark than the clouds. And if the heavy masses of ruined mountains or buildings fall into the vast pools of water, a great quantity will be flung into the air, and its movement will be in a contrary direction to that of the object which struck the water; that is to say, the angle of reflection will be equal to the angle of incidence.

187
Notes and sketches on a deluge, c.1517–18

Pen and ink on rough paper. 30.1 × 20.9 cm.
Melzi's *178* (verso). RCIN 912665

188

A tempest, c.1513–18

Black chalk, pen and ink, wash. 27.0 × 40.8 cm.
Melzi's *107*. RCIN 912376. (Detail shown pp. 208–9)

189 [OPPOSITE]

A deluge, c.1513–18

Black chalk, pen and ink, wash, offset red chalk.
15.7 × 20.3 cm. Melzi's *139*. RCIN 912379

In parallel with these writings, Leonardo produced a remarkable series of drawings of deluges. Many elements recur in both the descriptions and the drawings, but there is no direct illustrative relationship between the two, and it is not possible to arrange the drawings in a single narrative sequence: they were no doubt drawn for Leonardo's own satisfaction, each as a self-contained image. Their dense delicacy is characteristic of Leonardo's last years, and while they may have been produced over an extended period, it is likely that most were drawn in France.

The most elaborate of these deluge drawings can be seen in **188**. Among dense clouds, wind-gods hurl thunderbolts or blow the storm along with trumpets. A landslide peels away from the remains of a mountain

at upper right, falling into the waters that rush around its base, while at lower right the tempest overwhelms a party of horsemen who cower on the ground as broken trees fall among them. **189** is similar in concept, though no figures are present – a flood descends from the right and sweeps across a wooded plain to engulf the stands of trees to the left, with the careful addition of wash creating differing degrees of obscuration in the clouds.

Seven of the deluge drawings form a uniform set, almost identical in size and worked in black chalk from edge to edge. In two drawings (**190**, **191**) a city is seen in the distance, helpless before the storm that engulfs it. A fortress on a mountain at bottom right is intact in **190**, collapsing outwards in **192**, and just a bare stump in **191**. In several of the sheets a mountain fragments

into crystalline blocks and cascades in arcs onto the city or drowned landscape below.

A couple of drawings (**193**, **194**) show the landscape in close-up, with individual trees blasted by the storm yet clinging to the remains of rocks, the waters running in waves around their base. In the final drawings of the group (**195**, **196**) all solid matter has been pulverised and swept away, and the scene is dominated by great plumes of wind, water and (in **195**) lightning issuing from the clouds.

The final drawing of this sequence (**197**) is much more formally finished. Leonardo has entirely worked up the black chalk with pen and wash, freezing the scene and thereby draining it both of suggestive power and the vastness or indeterminate scale that the vaporous black chalk allowed.

190 [ABOVE]

A deluge, c.1517–18

Black chalk. 15.8 × 21.0 cm. Melzi's *143*.
RCIN 912385

191 [OPPOSITE]

A deluge, c.1517–18

Black chalk. 16.3 × 21.0 cm. Melzi's *145*.
RCIN 912378

192

A deluge, c.1517–18

Black chalk. 16.1 × 20.7 cm.
RCIN 912382

193

194

195

196

193 [PREVIOUS PAGES]

A deluge, c.1517–18

Black chalk. 16.1 × 21.0 cm. Melzi's *141*.
RCIN 912386

194

A deluge, c.1517–18

Black chalk. 15.8 × 20.3 cm. Melzi's *142*.
RCIN 912377

195

A deluge, c.1517–18

Black chalk, touches of pen.
16.5 × 20.4 cm. Melzi's *[14]7*. RCIN 912384

196

A deluge, c.1517–18

Black chalk. 15.8 × 21.0 cm. Melzi's *[1]46*.
RCIN 912383

197 [ABOVE]

A deluge, c.1517–18

Black chalk, pen and ink, wash.
16.2 × 20.3 cm. Melzi's *[14]4*. RCIN 912380

Detail of **198**

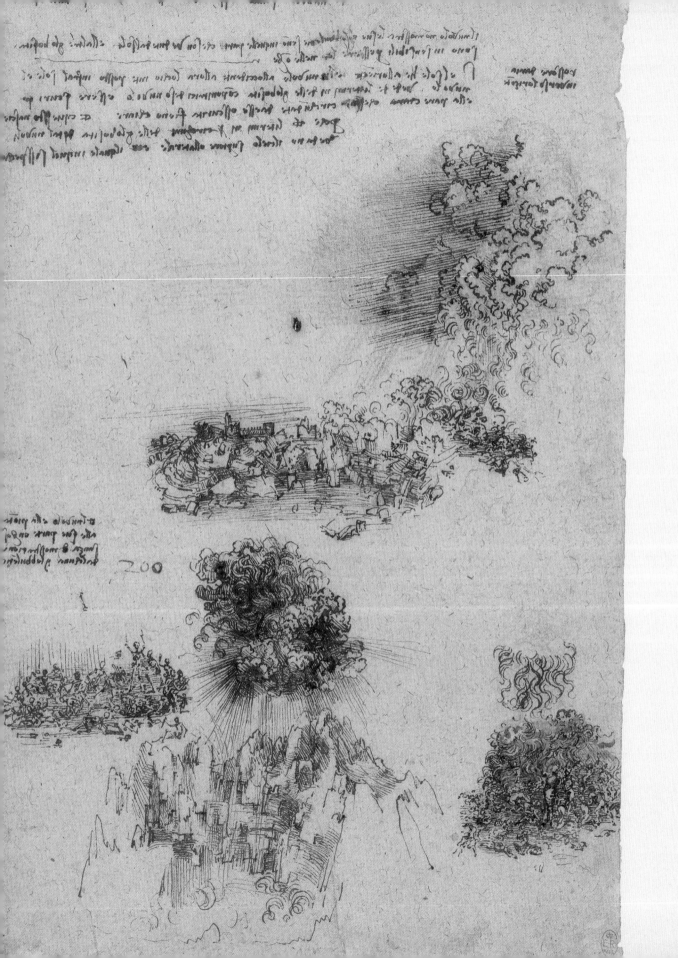

198

*Apocalyptic scenes,
with notes, c.1517–18*

Black chalk, pen and ink, wash, on rough paper.
30.0 × 20.3 cm. Melzi's *200*. RCIN 912388

A rather different subject matter is shown in **198**,
though the cataclysmic theme remains. Four separate
sketches show scenes from the end of the world: above,
fire rains down from a thundercloud onto tiny figures
as a mountain and fortress crumble into an abyss; a
great ball of smoke and fire burns over precipitous
cliffs surrounding a huge pit in which the sea boils;
to the right, cowering figures are incinerated by an
aerial fire, while to the left skeletons climb from their
graves. Many possible sources have been suggested –
the most obvious would be the last book of the Bible,
Revelation (or Apocalypse), but there is little direct
relationship between the images and specific passages
from Revelation. Towards the end of his life Leonardo
had accumulated such a rich personal iconography of
catastrophe and destruction that he had no need to
follow another's writings. Once again, the notes on the
sheet are coolly scientific, discussing the appearance of
sunlit clouds (cf. **29**, **199**).

199

A study of clouds, c.1518

Black chalk or charcoal on paper rubbed with the same,
pen and ink. 29.0 × 19.5 cm. Melzi's *135*. RCIN 912391

Leonardo's technique of red chalk on red prepared
paper reached its logical conclusion, at the end of his
life, in a small group of sheets executed in black chalk
(or possibly charcoal) on paper rubbed all over with the
same medium, or prepared with a dark grey coating;
one bears the date 24 June 1518, the latest date written
by Leonardo in any of his notes. The rubbing-in of the
chalk made the surface of the paper smoother and the
drawing more vulnerable to abrasion, and Leonardo's
study here has been largely effaced. But three layers of
stratiform clouds can be discerned in the upper half of
the sheet, and two formations of cumuliform clouds
to centre and lower left, possibly with mountain peaks
below. The note reads 'The shadows in clouds are lighter
in proportion as they are nearer to the horizon.'

200

The head of an old bearded man in profile, c.1519

Black chalk on rough paper. 25.3 × 18.2 cm.
Melzi's 47. RCIN 912500

In October 1517, Cardinal Luigi of Aragon visited Leonardo in his studio in France. His secretary Antonio de Beatis recorded that Leonardo was more than 70 years old (he was actually 65) and that 'a certain paralysis has crippled his right hand'.[29] If this is true, it would have prevented Leonardo from large-scale or physically demanding work, but most of the drawings and notes (made with his left hand) from his French years are as firm and controlled as at any point of his life.

This drawing is different. It is the last of Leonardo's 'ideal heads' (160–165), on a thick, mealy, low-quality paper, and though its rough surface contributes to the broken nature of the chalk lines, they are clearly more hesitant, suggesting that he was no longer fully in control of his chalk. It must have been drawn right at the end of Leonardo's life, as his physical powers started to fail him.

An old bearded man drawing an old bearded man cannot have been oblivious to an element of self-portraiture, even self-caricature, but there is nothing comic about the image. While the old man in **165** (drawn just a year or two earlier) has a strong neck and firm features, here the lank hair, rheumy eyes, peg-like teeth and pendulous nose surely express Leonardo's feelings about his own decay. Melzi's portrait of Leonardo (**1**) shows that he retained a fine profile into old age, and this is not a literal self-portrait. But it must be regarded on a profound level as a self-image, an exploration of Leonardo's perception of himself, both noble and pathetic, as he approached death.

From 1 February to 6 May 2019,
the selections of drawings on
the following pages are exhibited
at museums and galleries across
the United Kingdom.

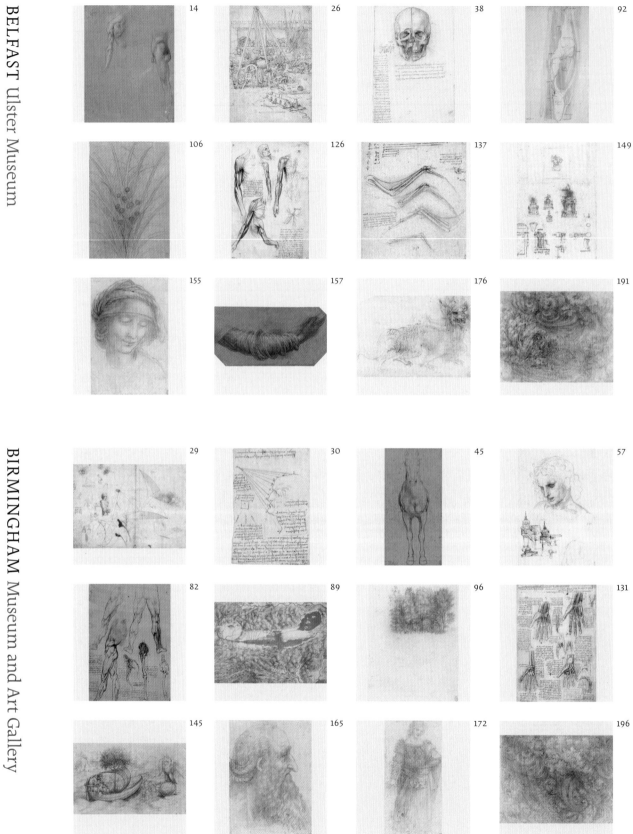

14

26

38

92

106

126

137

149

155

157

176

191

29

30

45

57

82

89

96

131

145

165

172

196

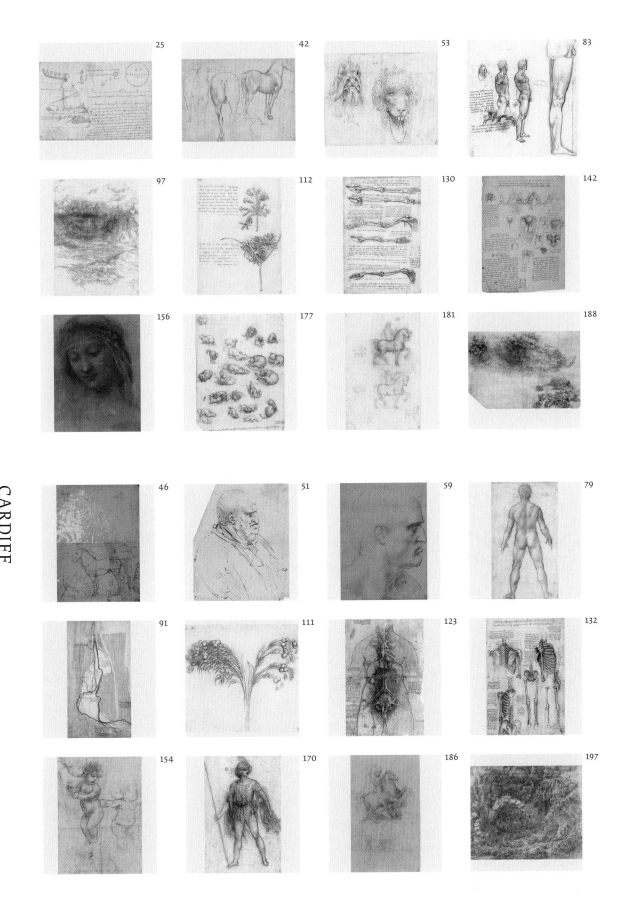

25 42 53 83 97 112 130 142 156 177 181 188 46 51 59 79 91 111 123 132 154 170 186 197

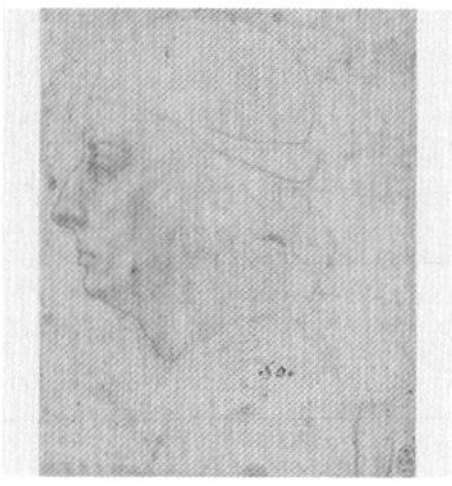

12

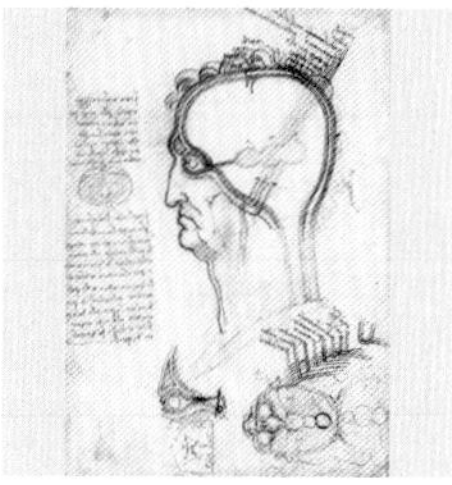

39

65

68

74

95

110

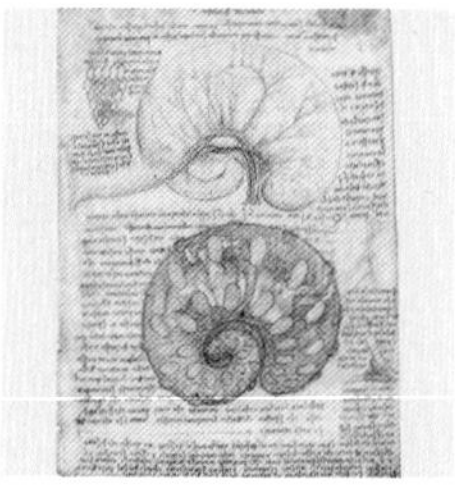

122

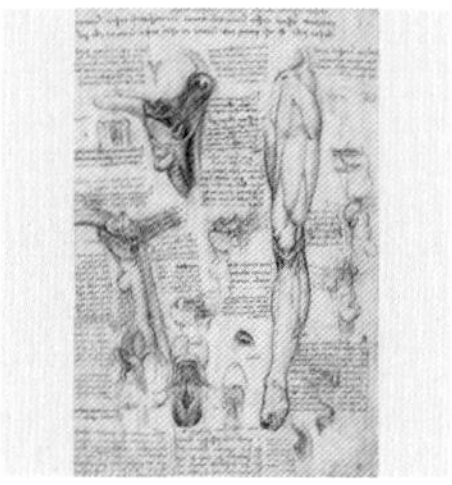

135

146

162

194

21

36

52

64

86

102

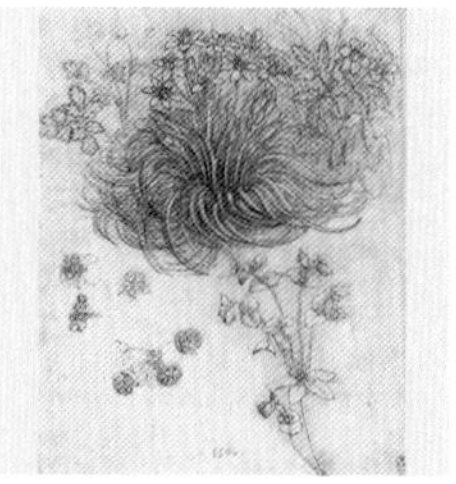

105

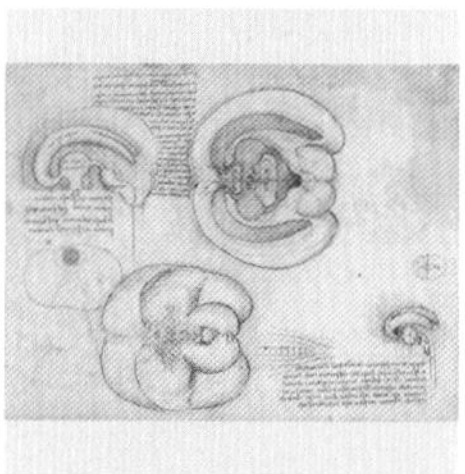

124

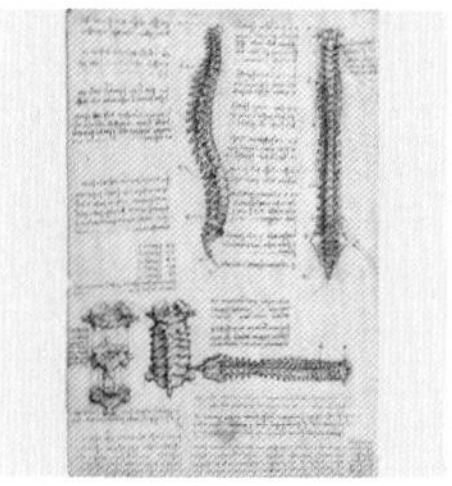

133

174

182

192

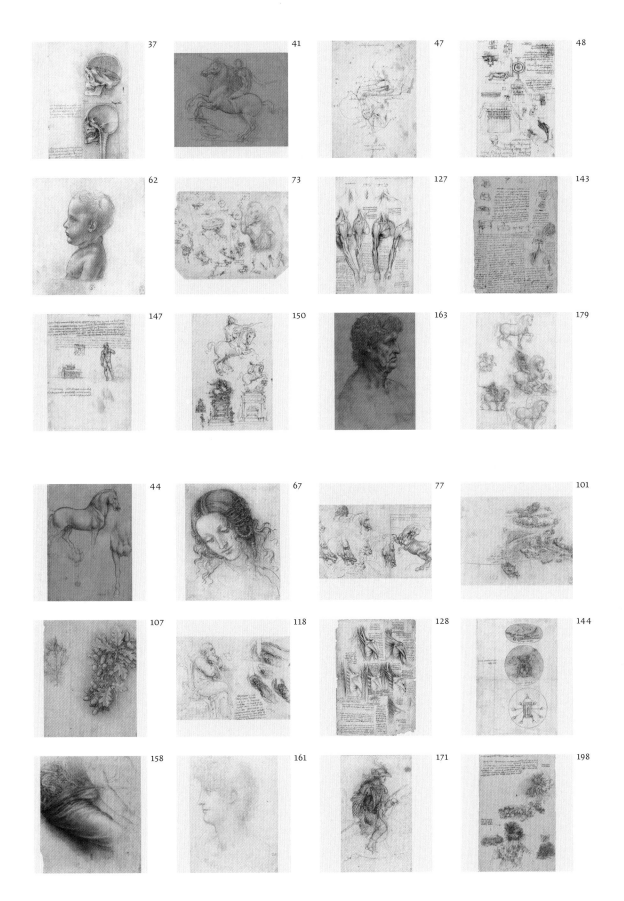

37 41 47 48

62 73 127 143

147 150 163 179

44 67 77 101

107 118 128 144

158 161 171 198

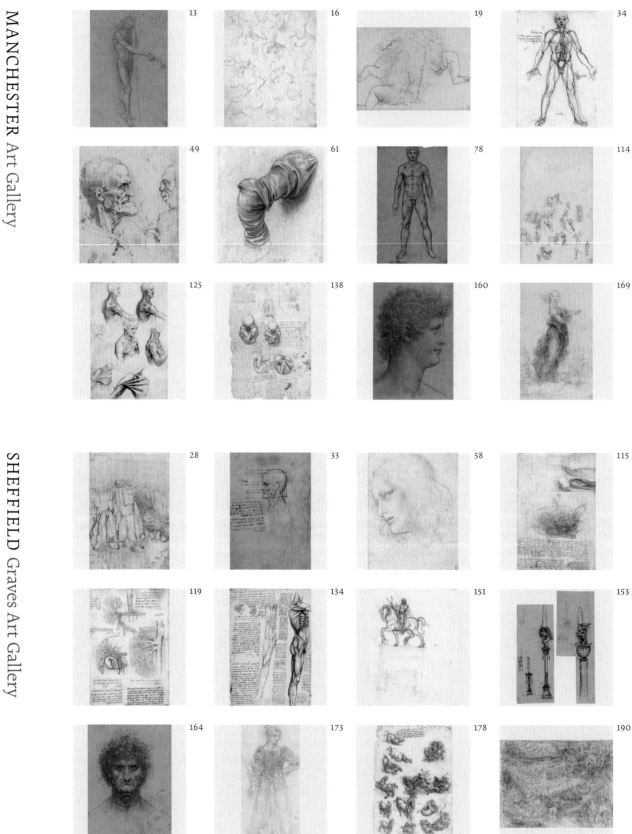

13
16
19
34
49
61
78
114
125
138
160
169

28
33
58
115
119
134
151
153
164
173
178
190

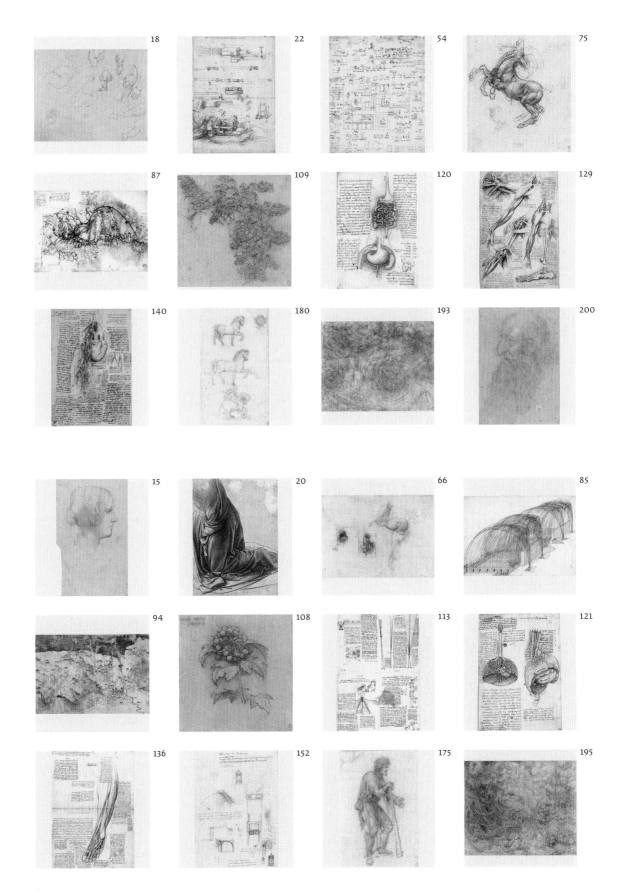

SOUTHAMPTON City Art Gallery

SUNDERLAND Museum and Winter Gardens

Further reading

All of Leonardo's drawings at Windsor are catalogued and reproduced in Kenneth Clark and Carlo Pedretti, *The Drawings of Leonardo da Vinci in the Collection of Her Majesty The Queen at Windsor Castle* (3 vols, London 1968–9), and can be studied on Royal Collection Trust's website, www.rct.uk

The other major collection of Leonardo's drawings, the Codex Atlanticus in the Biblioteca Ambrosiana, Milan, has been published twice in facsimile, more recently as *Il Codice Atlantico di Leonardo da Vinci* (12 vols, Florence 1973–5), with a transcription in a further 12 vols by Augusto Marinoni (Florence 1975) and an independent catalogue in 2 vols by Carlo Pedretti (London and New York 1978). All of Leonardo's notebooks have also been published in facsimile.

The best compendium of Leonardo's writings is Jean Paul Richter, *The Literary Works of Leonardo da Vinci* (3rd edn, 2 vols, London and New York 1970), to be read in conjunction with Carlo Pedretti, *The Literary Works of Leonardo da Vinci: A Commentary to Jean Paul Richter's Edition* (2 vols, Oxford 1977). The most coherent reconstruction of Leonardo's planned treatise is Martin Kemp and Margaret Walker, *Leonardo on Painting* (New Haven and London 1989).

The literature on Leonardo is immense, and the following list contains only a handful of the more satisfactory and readily available books in English on the artist:

CARMEN BAMBACH *et al.*
Leonardo da Vinci: Master Draftsman, New York 2003

KENNETH CLARK
Leonardo da Vinci: An Account of his Development as an Artist, Cambridge 1939 (and later editions)

MARTIN CLAYTON
Leonardo da Vinci: The Divine and the Grotesque, London 2002

MARTIN CLAYTON AND RON PHILO
Leonardo da Vinci: Anatomist, London 2012

ALAN DONNITHORNE
Leonardo da Vinci: A Closer Look, London 2019

PAOLO GALLUZZI (ed.)
Leonardo da Vinci: Engineer and Architect, Montreal 1987

WALTER ISAACSON
Leonardo da Vinci, New York 2017

JONATHAN JONES
The Lost Battles: Leonardo, Michelangelo and the Artistic Duel that Defined the Renaissance, London 2010

MARTIN KEMP
Leonardo da Vinci: The Marvellous Works of Nature and Man, London 1981

Leonardo da Vinci: Experience, Experiment and Design, London 2006

MARTIN KEMP, JANE ROBERTS *et al.*
Leonardo da Vinci: Artist, Scientist, Inventor, London 1989

MARTIN KEMP AND GIUSEPPE PALLANTI
Mona Lisa: The People and the Painting, Oxford 2017

ROSS KING
Leonardo and the Last Supper, London 2013

PIETRO MARANI
Leonardo da Vinci: The Complete Paintings, New York 2000

PIETRO MARANI, MARIA TERESA FIORIO *et al.*
Leonardo da Vinci: The Design of the World, Milan 2015

CHARLES NICHOLL
Leonardo da Vinci: The Flights of the Mind, London 2004

CARLO PEDRETTI
Leonardo da Vinci: Nature Studies from the Royal Library at Windsor Castle, London 1981

Leonardo da Vinci: Studies for the Last Supper from the Royal Library at Windsor Castle, Milan 1983

Leonardo da Vinci: Drawings of Horses from the Royal Library at Windsor Castle, Florence 1984

Leonardo: Architect, London 1986

A.E. POPHAM
The Drawings of Leonardo da Vinci, London 1946 (and later editions)

LUKE SYSON *et al.*
Leonardo da Vinci: Painter at the Court of Milan, London 2011

FRANK ZÖLLNER AND JOHANNES NATHAN
Leonardo da Vinci: The Complete Paintings and Drawings, Cologne 2003

Notes

1 Kemp 1981, p. 349.

2 Ludwig Goldscheider, *Leonardo da Vinci*, London 1959, p. 32.

3 Giorgio Vasari, *Delle vite de' piu eccellenti pittori scultori et architettori*, Florence 1568, II, p. 7.

4 Edoardo Villata, *Leonardo da Vinci. I documenti e le testimonianze contemporanee*, Milan 1999, p. 276.

5 British Library, MS Sloane 1906, ff. 3r–v.

6 Richter 1970, no. 585.

7 Paris MS B, f.10.r.

8 Richter 1970, no. 1340.

9 Villata 1999, p. 44.

10 Richter 1970, no. 720.

11 Richter 1970, no. 1345.

12 Dante, *Inferno*, XXIV: 49–51.

13 Villata 1999, p. 136.

14 Villata 1999, p. 203.

15 Ladislao Reti, 'The two unpublished manuscripts of Leonardo da Vinci in the Biblioteca Nacional of Madrid – II', *Burlington Magazine* CX, 1968, p. 81.

16 Richter 1970, no. 602.

17 Richter 1970, no. 393.

18 Richter 1970, no. 1060.

19 Richter 1970, no. 680; Vasari, 1568, II, p. 5.

20 Richter 1970, no. 368.

21 RCIN 919027v; Clayton and Philo 2012, p. 82.

22 Villata 1999, p. 135.

23 Vasari, 1568, II, p. 8.

24 Ibid.

25 Syson *et al.* 2011, p. 45.

26 Vasari 1568, II, p. 8.

27 British Library, MS Harley 3462, ff. 249v–255r.

28 Richter 1970, no. 825.

29 Villata 1999, p. 263.

ISBN Hardback 978 1 909741 47 8
ISBN Paperback 978 1 909741 66 9
Hardback 101521
Paperback 101522
British Library Cataloguing in Publication data: A catalogue record of this book is available from the British Library

Designer Sally McIntosh
Project manager Elizabeth Silverton
Edited by Sarah Kane
Colour reproduction Mercator Fonds
Printed and bound in Belgium by Die Keure

This catalogue has been published with generous support from the Gilbert and Ildiko Butler Family Foundation Inc.

Published 2018 by Royal Collection Trust
York House, St James's Palace
London SW1A 1BQ

Index

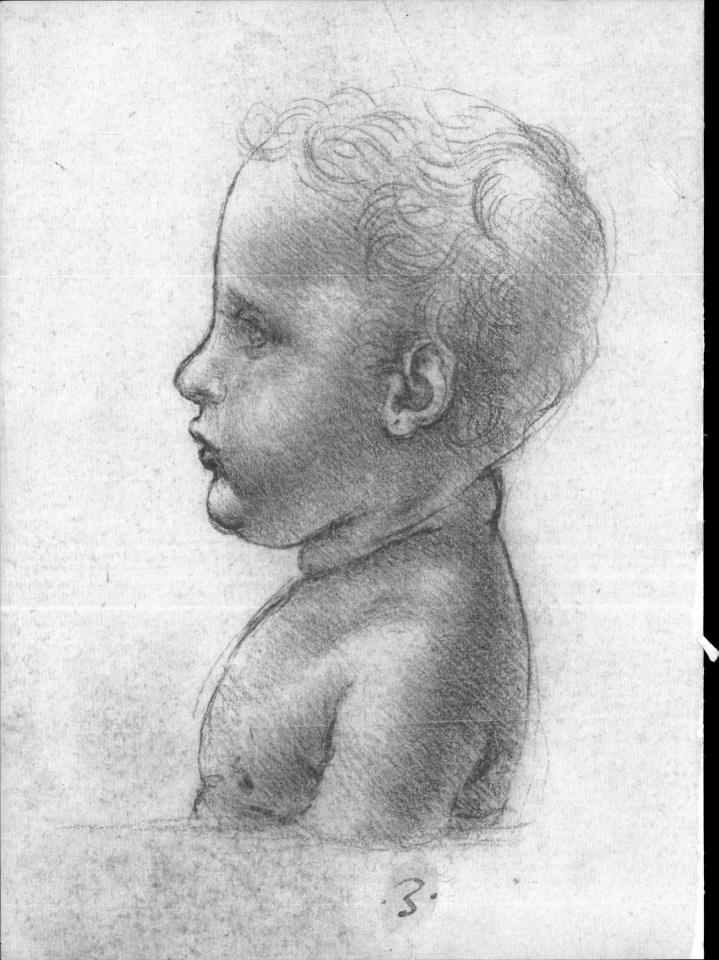